·PARIS·
A CITY REVEALED

METRO BOOKS
New York

An Imprint of Sterling Publishing
387 Park Avenue South
New York, NY 10016

Written by Mike Gerrard and Donna Dailey
Senior Editor: Donna Wood
Senior Designer: Carole Philp
Picture Researcher: Michelle Aylott
Image retouching and internal repro: Michael Moody

ISBN 978-1-4351-0510-2

For information about custom editions, special sales, and premium and corporate purchases, please contact Sterling Special Sales at 800-805-5489 or specialsales@sterlingpublishing.com.

Manufactured in China by C & C Offset Printing Co., Ltd

4 6 8 10 9 7 5

www.sterlingpublishing.com

The AA's website address is theAA.com/shop

PAGE 1: *Nôtre-Dame Cathedral, 170 years in the building*
PAGES 2–3: *More noted for its stained glass, Sainte-Chapelle also has beautifully intricate carvings*
PAGES 4–5: *The Gothic Gare de l'Est, where time seems to have stood still*

Contents

The Islands &
the River Seine

Most cities begin with a river. Paris, the City of Light, could just as easily be the City of Water. It was here, where the Seine flows past two islands, that a tribe called the Parisii settled and founded a fishing village in about 250BC. Older human remains have also been found, along with the remnants of dug-out canoes, showing that this has been a crossing-point for several thousand years.

It is here that you will find Paris's oldest still-standing bridge, the Pont Neuf, or New Bridge. It joins the left and right banks of the Seine, crossing over the tip of the Île de la Cité as it does so, and it dates back to 1578, when King Henri III laid the first stone. The bridge has been recently renovated but looks pretty much as it did when it was first built 400 years ago.

It's on the Île de la Cité that you'll find Paris's grand cathedral, Nôtre-Dame, whose origins go back even further than the Pont Neuf, as the first stone was put down in the 12th century. Nearby, work on the Conciergerie, originally a royal palace, began in the 14th century, while the stunning chapel of Sainte-Chapelle goes back to the 13th century. All can still be visited: a testimony to medieval building skills indeed.
The Seine is comparatively shallow and slow-flowing at this point, making it ideal for navigation and for trade. It glides on past Rouen, the ancient capital of Normandy, and on to its mouth at Le Havre, where it connects Paris with the oceans of the world.

Graceful house fronts overlook the Seine, and
Nôtre-Dame towers over these Paris houses

La Conciergerie

This island in the Seine had been the home of the Kings of France since the 10th century, and the Conciergerie was built as a huge royal palace by Philippe le Bel in 1301–15. It became a prison, the role for which it is best known, in the late 14th century after the royal household had crossed the Seine into the new Louvre Palace.

The Conciergerie remained a prison for around 500 years, till 1914, but is famed for that short period during the French Revolution when aristocratic prisoners were held here before being sent to the guillotine. More than 4,000 passed through its gates in the early 1790s, one of these being Marie Antoinette, and visitors can still see the tiny cell in which she was held.

In contrast, the vast Salle des Gens d'Armes is 206ft (63m) long and its vaulted ceilings are 28ft (8.5m) high. Some 2,000 members of the royal household used to dine here, and directly above are the kitchens, which can still be visited. There are four fireplaces, each big enough to roast two sheep in. The Salle des Gens d'Armes is thought to be the oldest surviving medieval hall in Europe. Today, concerts are sometimes held there, a stunning setting and a hark back to its original function when it was a royal palace, built to impress.

BELOW *At night, there are strong memories of when the Conciergerie was a prison*

RIGHT *The impressive Salle des Gens d'Armes evokes grander times*

Île de la Cité

RIGHT *The Île de la Cité by night beckons visitors to its back streets*

BELOW *By day, from across the River Seine, traces of its history are far more evident*

If the Seine were suddenly to dry up, the Île de la Cité would be seen as a kind of medieval fortress, rising up from the land around it and filled with most of the important features any such city would have needed: a cathedral, a palace of justice, a royal palace that became a prison, chapels, narrow back streets and all kinds of accommodation, for rich and poor alike.

It's on this island that the Parisii tribe are first thought to have settled, although there's some speculation that in those days, about 52BC, there was another island on the river which has now disappeared. At the time the area was certainly subject to flooding, and when the Romans came they chose to make their base on the Left Bank, though they sought refuge on the Île de la Cité when attacked by the Huns.

If it was the location of the founding of Paris, it remains today not just at the heart of the city but at the heart of the country. Set in the cobbles in front of Nôtre-Dame Cathedral is the 'zero kilometre' point, from which all road distances from Paris are measured. Several bridges link the island to the rest of the city, although they no longer carry housing as many once did. The first stone bridge was built in 1378, linking the island to the Left Bank, but 30 years later it was swept away like the *Titanic* by ice floes that thundered down the river, taking the bridge, the houses and the people with them.

In the evening, lighting gives the island an almost magical glow. One of the best ways to appreciate its beautiful architecture is by boat, taking one of the trips that start from below the Pont Neuf, Paris's oldest bridge. From the water you'll see the elegant Nôtre-Dame rising high above the banks, and the stern façade of the Conciergerie, once Paris's most notorious prison. These days the island is a rather safer and more sedate place to be. Much of the original housing has gone to make way for the Palace of Justice and other government buildings, including the police headquarters that would be familiar to readers of Simenon's Inspector Maigret novels. Explore the remaining back streets, though, and you will find chic shops and ancient shops, side by side, and a part of Paris still with an atmosphere all of its own.

OPPOSITE *The Île Saint-Louis provides visitors with the archetypal riverbank view of Paris*

LEFT *Flowers are for sale here as well as at the more famous Marché aux Fleurs (Flower Market) on the adjoining Île de la Cité*

BELOW *The quieter island streets are more conducive to cycling*

Île Saint-Louis

The Île Saint-Louis is the more homely of the two islands on the Seine. Too small to allow the building of grand edifices like Nôtre-Dame or the Conciergerie, it has traditionally been a desirable residential area, and remains so to this day. It's a beautiful place for a stroll, as many Parisians know, and its narrow streets are lined with galleries, restaurants, specialist shops and boutique hotels. The fact that the island has no Métro station adds to its air of exclusivity among the locals.

There are several handsome mansions that were designed by Louis Le Vau, one of the leading architects of his day. Le Vau also produced the designs for the church of Saint-Louis en l'Île, which was begun in 1664 to replace an earlier chapel that was now too small to cope with the growing island population. The architect lived at 3 quai d'Anjou, which is on the northeast side of the island, and another distinguished resident also lived here, at number 9, the artist Honoré Daumier. A walk from here around the eastern tip of the island, the place Antoine-Louis Barye (named after the sculptor) is rewarding as it leads to lovely views of the Left Bank.

It was only in the 17th century that the Île Saint-Louis as we know it actually came into being, as until then it was two separate islands that were joined together. The new island was linked to the smart and expensive area of the Marais on the Right Bank by the building of the Pont Marie in 1635, which was named after the man who developed the Île Saint-Louis, Christophe Marie. Then, as now, new areas of an expanding city were ripe for development. The Île Saint-Louis is linked to the Île de la Cité by the Pont Saint-Louis, which was originally built in 1614 but needed to be replaced in 1969.

15

Sainte-Chapelle

One of the most breathtaking views in Paris is the moment when you walk for the first time into the upper part of the church of Sainte-Chapelle. It has the largest area of stained glass anywhere in the world, and is all the more remarkable for being in such a comparatively small space. The effect on a fine day when the sun is streaming through the windows can be overwhelming.

Sainte-Chapelle (Holy Chapel) was built by the only French king to have been canonized, King Louis IX, who became St Louis and gave his name to the adjoining island, Île Saint-Louis. King Louis went off on the Crusades and brought back with him various alleged relics including the Crown of Thorns, some drops of Christ's blood and a nail from the cross. He built Sainte-Chapelle in 1248 to house these relics.

The stained glass windows in the upper chapel tell the stories of the Bible, from the Creation to the Apocalypse, in 1,134 separate scenes. A staircase leads today's visitors up to the glory of the upper chapel, where the royal family prayed, and where the 15 windows stretch up to 49ft (15m) high, enhanced by an imposing rose window. About two-thirds of the glass is the original work from the 12th-century construction, which makes it the oldest stained glass in Paris. The only non-Biblical story is in the final window, which shows how King Louis brought back the relics from the Crusades.

ABOVE *Sainte-Chapelle is striking from the outside but nothing prepares the visitor for its interior, shown in the main picture*

BELOW *Stained glass windows such as this tell the story of St-Etienne du Mont, and bathe the upper chapel in light. They are among the city's most impressive sights*

Nôtre-Dame de Paris

There is a greater sense of Paris's history at Nôtre-Dame than anywhere else in the city. The atmosphere, like the building itself, is monumental. Its foundation stone was laid in 1163 and for the next 170 years several thousand craftsmen, often from the same family, laboured to produce this cathedral dedicated to Our Lady. It is the spiritual centre of the whole nation, where kings and emperors have been crowned, where Popes have prayed, where presidents have been laid to rest, where Joan of Arc was put on trial, and which has inspired artists and writers and today inspires over 10 million visitors each year.

The significance of the building is evident from the laying of that very first foundation stone, which was carried out by Pope Alexander III. The original building was designed by Bishop Maurice de Sully, who made innovative use of flying buttresses. These allowed for the construction of much higher and thinner walls than had ever been needed before, giving Nôtre-Dame a magnificent sense of space, calmness and grandeur. The best views of the buttresses and the building as a whole can be had from the back rather than the front of the cathedral and from the river. Some boat trips on the Seine include a circular tour around the island, and the size and scale of the construction are very evident from the water.

RIGHT *The grandeur of the cathedral of Nôtre-Dame is particularly evident when viewing the building at night*

BELOW *Every detail is a testimony to the craftsmen who laboured to complete this monumental work*

The most familiar view is of the symmetrical West Front, the main entrance to the cathedral. Its three entrance arches, impressive enough by themselves, are dwarfed by the vast twin towers that rise some 226ft (69m) towards the heavens. The three entrance arches and other sculptures and carvings were intended as a visual telling of the Bible, built in days when the vast majority of the population was illiterate. One arch tells the story of the life of St Anne, another the story of the Last Judgement, and the most impressive of all is the 13th-century Portal of the Virgin. This depicts the life and death of the Virgin Mary, and her Ascension and crowning in heaven.

Above these entrance portals is a row of 28 statues representing various Biblical figures, although during the French Revolution these were mistakenly thought by the revolutionaries to be the French kings. The heads were cut off and what can be seen today are 19th-century replicas.

The most famous heads in the cathedral are probably those of the gargoyles, which were added to the building by architect Viollet-le-Duc to ward off evil during the 1841–64 reconstruction of Nôtre-Dame. This was necessary because the destruction wrought by the revolutionaries resulted in the entire building almost being destroyed. The world today owes a great debt of gratitude to the writer Victor Hugo, who campaigned to have it restored to its original glory. When his book *Nôtre-Dame de Paris*, which is better known outside France by its English title, *The Hunchback of Nôtre-Dame*, was published in 1831, the cathedral was in a very sorry state of repair. The success of the book, and of Hugo's tireless campaign, ensured that the French government stepped in and began the 23-year restoration of Nôtre-Dame.

Not even the pomp and ceremony of the coronation of Emperor Napoleon in Nôtre-Dame in 1804 was enough to warrant the huge reconstruction programme that was necessary. Parts of the damaged building were concealed behind curtains and screens. Other coronations in the cathedral included those of King Henry VI of England in 1430, and King Francois II and his wife Mary Stuart (Mary Queen of Scots) in 1559.

OPPOSITE *The carved portals at the main entrance to Nôtre-Dame, on its West Front, would by themselves take the visitor hours to fully enjoy, before even venturing in to see the grand interior*

BELOW *The central nave soars to a height of 115ft (35m)*

Central Paris

If Paris began on the islands in the river, its centre shifted to the Right Bank in the 13th century, when King Philippe Auguste ordered a defensive fortress to be built here. This eventually became a royal palace (and later the Musée du Louvre), and as the royal family moved from the Île de la Cité, so too did much of the life of the city. By the time the royal court moved out to the new grand palace at Versailles in the 17th century, this area was established as the heart of Paris.

The city's main market, Les Halles, had been on the right bank since the 12th century, but later other significant aspects of Parisian life would be found here, ranging from the opera and the Commercial Exchange to the Folies Bergère. More recently still, the controversial Centre Georges Pompidou was built, the infamous 'inside-out' art gallery and cultural centre.

The nature of the buildings here is indicative of the contrast of the Parisian character: a love of the traditional and classical combined with a need to be at the cutting-edge of modernity. The 17th-century Palais-Royal has a courtyard filled with modern sculpture.

The Orangerie Gallery, which is renowned for its displays of Monet's waterlily paintings, exists almost side-by-side with the newly revamped Jeu de Paume, specializing in contemporary displays of video installations and other visual arts. It's a reminder that, in his time, Monet and some of his fellow Impressionist painters were regarded as scandalously *avant-garde*, just as some of the displays in today's Jeu de Paume are. Paris embraces both, here in the very centre of the city.

The upper floors of the Pompidou Centre provide a superb panoramic view of the centre of the city

23

Bourse de Commerce

The Bourse de Commerce, or Commercial Exchange, is the only survivor of the city's main market, Les Halles (see pages 32-33), which had been here since 1183. The Bourse de Commerce – not to be confused with La Bourse, or the Stock Exchange – was built in 1767 as a Corn Exchange. The distinctive round building was given its metal-framed dome in 1811, and was further modernized in 1888.

The dome was originally wooden, and this was then replaced with an iron dome, then a copper dome, and finally the mix of metal and glass that we see today, and which is so typical of many Paris buildings of the same period. Gustave Eiffel produced many such structures using metal and glass, and they were far more typical of his work than the Eiffel Tower which bears his name. The dome of the Bourse was not an Eiffel creation, but certainly could have been from its appearance.

It is still an active Commercial Exchange, concentrating on the coffee and sugar markets, and it also houses the Paris Chamber of Commerce and Industry as well as the Paris headquarters of the World Trade Centre.

RIGHT *Almost 250 years old, the Bourse de Commerce has been modernized since it was first built but still retains its original look*

BELOW *The metal dome (partly visible in the background) was added in 1811*

Centre Georges Pompidou

Known familiarly as the Pompidou Centre, the full name of this splendid modern creation is the Centre National d'Art et de Culture Georges-Pompidou. It sometimes seems as if there is as much fun to be had outside the building as inside, and the building was certainly designed to be as striking from the exterior as from the interior. It caused great controversy when it was opened in 1977 for its 'inside-out' appearance, with multi-coloured pipes and ducts snaking up the walls, a modern creation disrupting the classical elegance of the city of Paris. But then, many people said the same about the Eiffel Tower when it was built, and now it is the icon of the city. The Pompidou Centre is not far behind and is one of the most easily recognized buildings in the world.

The centre was the brainchild of Georges Pompidou, who was President of France from 1969 until 1974. He was a man of vision, though these were not always successful. He was also responsible for the creation of the Tour Montparnasse (see pages 150-151), though he was not totally pleased with that result. The art centre that bears his name has been a triumph, however, and has

FAR RIGHT *At first glance the Pompidou Centre still looks unfinished, as if it's behind scaffolding and behind schedule, but the building was completed in 1977 and the industrial look is deliberate*

RIGHT *The playful Firebird fountains in the place Igor-Stravinsky, beside the building, leave no doubt that this is a home for modern art*

achieved one of the President's aims, which was to revitalize the Beaubourg area, so close to the city centre and yet in the 1960s rather run-down and shabby. Pompidou also wanted to create a centre where people could experience all kinds of modern art, including permanent and temporary exhibitions, concerts, dance, drama, movies, as well as enjoy a comprehensive and accessible library (which remains open into the evening, when more people are free to use it).

The architects were Richard Rogers and Renzo Piano, and their bold idea was to turn the building inside-out, to make a colourful feature of the parts of a building that are usually dull and hidden from view. So, bright blue pipes carry the air-conditioning, green indicates water pipes, the electrical cables are inside the vivid yellow pipes, and the escalator that carries people up the front of the building, on the outside, is bright red underneath.

In contrast to the busyness of the building, the big square in front has been left largely open, with one or two dramatically placed sculptures. The area is never quiet, as it is a natural magnet for people to relax in for a while, grab a picnic or a cup of coffee, and enjoy the busking musicians, mime artists, fire-eaters and other forms of street theatre.

Around the corner from the fire-eaters, at the side of the building, are the Firebird fountains. Inspired by Stravinsky's 1910 ballet *The Firebird*, these fountains match the bold primary colours of the exterior of the Pompidou Centre. They also match its sense of playfulness, and the message that art can be fun, by swivelling and swirling and spraying water around the place, to the delight of both children and adults.

Inside the building are all the elements President Georges Pompidou wanted to see – cinemas, galleries, bookshops, library, cafés. The main draw for many visitors is the Musée Nationale d'Art Moderne, which occupies two of the building's six floors. It is the third part of the city's trilogy of art museums, after the Louvre and the Musée d'Orsay, taking over where the Musée d'Orsay's collection stops, in 1905. Here in the Pompidou Centre are works by Picasso, Matisse, Miró, Braque, Warhol, Pollock and many more. About 2,000 items from the 50,000-strong collection are on display at any one time, although these normally include some of the major highlights such as Braque's *Man with a Guitar* and Miró's *Blues* – both works that seem perfectly at home in Pompidou's outrageous cultural centre.

Folies-Bergère

As much as it is a city of art, food and architecture, Paris is a city of love, romance and sex. Men propose on top of the Eiffel Tower, lovers stroll by the Seine, and the extra-marital affairs of politicians and TV celebrities are thought of as normal rather than reasons for them to resign from their jobs. Paris has also always been a city that has the glitz of fashion and the pizzazz of jazz and showbiz. Sew all these threads together and the inevitable result is the dazzling over-the-top cabaret show featuring scantily clad girls – and men – doing production numbers that are always tastefully erotic.

The Moulin Rouge is one of the best known shows for its association with the artists of Montmartre, but 20 years before it opened its doors in 1889, the Folies-Bergère was already in business, right in the city centre. It opened in 1869 and remains open today, almost 150 years later,

testament to the well-known fact that sex, glitz and titillation never go out of fashion.

The style of the fashions change, though, with the times. The Folies began with risqué shows combining satire with sex, which is not surprising as it took over the site of the Café Sommier Elastique, or the Springy Mattress Café. By the 1920s and 30s it had become more of an all-round cabaret, featuring popular singers like Maurice Chevalier but also the erotic arts of the legendary Josephine Baker, renowned for her semi-nude dances.

In the 1950s, with the arrival of rivals like the Crazy Horse, the Folies competed with its lines of topless dancers, after the style of the Lido's famous Bluebell Girls. Today the Folies has changed yet again, providing Broadway-style musicals but with, of course, an added veneer of sex. Paris wouldn't be Paris without it.

ABOVE *Most people associate the Folies-Bergère with the human shapes inside*

RIGHT *The outside and the public areas of this 1869 building also have many stylish lines to admire, bringing both grace and glamour to the Paris nightlife*

PAGE 31 *The brightly lit entrance to the building still draws the crowds*

Les Halles

Between 1183 and 1870, the area of Les Halles was one of the greatest markets in Europe, if not the world, and its mix of trade, crime, food, death, history, noise, colour and squalor inspired writers and artists. They included Victor Hugo, who vividly described Les Halles in his 1862 novel about the poor of Paris, *Les Misérables*, and the city's other great chronicler, Emile Zola. Zola called it *le ventre de Paris*, or the belly of Paris.

In Zola's time the market was at its height, with 10 new huge pavilions having been built in the 1860s. But the market's days were numbered, as the city grew and the narrow city-centre streets around Les Halles simply could not cope with the increase of traffic and the huge deliveries needed to satisfy the city's traders. In 1969 the market, almost 800 years old, was moved out to a new modern home in Rungis, with many saying that the heart – and the belly – had been ripped out of Paris.

The replacement Forum des Halles is a huge and confusing shopping centre, not especially attractive and with mass-market shops, fed by the combination Métro and RER station beneath, which is the largest in the world. On the positive side, the opening up of the market area has meant that some of the district's fine buildings, including the church of St-Eustache (left), can be seen and admired properly for the first time in centuries. The streets around, like the cobbled rue Montorgueil, do retain some of the atmosphere of Les Halles of old.

ABOVE *The Paris market at Les Halles has long been converted into a modern shopping centre, but there is still drama, as this night-time shot shows*

LEFT *This dominant building is the vast Gothic and Renaissance church of St-Eustache, which has filled the Paris skyline since it was built in 1637*

Musée du Louvre

The Louvre is more – much more – than one of the finest art collections in the world. It is an art object in itself, or rather a collection of them from ancient to modern. It is not only a repository of historical objects, it is an observer of history too, the history of Paris. Some of the best things about the Louvre are not hanging on its walls or standing on pedestals, they are beneath the building, within its fabric, and outside it too.

Its history goes back over 800 years, to 1190 when King Philippe-Auguste built a fortress on this spot, parts of which can still be seen down below the present building. The bases of some towers and the drawbridge support were unearthed in the 1980s and now provide a dramatic display deep beneath more famous aspects of the Louvre like the *Mona Lisa* and *Venus de Milo*.

In the 14th century the building became more than just a fortress, it became a royal palace when Charles V moved his court here from where it had been based on the Île de la Cité (see pages 12-13). The next major development was in the 16th century, when King François I started afresh and built a new Renaissance-style royal palace here, and also began the royal art collection. The whole magnificent Louvre collection of over 350,000 objects began with just 12 paintings that had been stolen from Italy. It was King François who brought not only the famous *Mona Lisa* but also the young artist, Leonardo da Vinci, to Paris for the first time.

The Louvre stopped being a royal palace when Louis XIV moved the court out to his new and overwhelmingly sumptuous palace at Versailles in the 17th century. The result of this move and the ostentatious display of royal wealth was the French Revolution, and it was the revolutionaries who, in 1793, opened a part of the Louvre to the public as the Musée de la République so that everyone might enjoy what had been until then the private royal art collection.

In 1810 Napoleon I married Marie-Louise in the Louvre, and began extending the buildings although he himself lived in the nearby Tuileries Palace. Those extensions were needed as the art collection expanded dramatically thanks to the plundering during Napoleon's various victories around Europe.

By the early 1980s it had become obvious that the Louvre was bursting at the seams, and there was insufficient space for both the increasing numbers of visitors and to display more than a fraction of the vast collection. In 1983 the *Grand Projet du Louvre* began, which involved acquiring a new wing by ejecting the Ministry of Finance, though the most controversial aspect involved the building of a glass pyramid in the courtyard.

Paris has never shied away from the controversial in matters of art and architecture, with the Eiffel Tower and the Pompidou Centre being other examples that shocked some and excited others. That too was the case with the pyramid, designed by the Chinese-American architect I.M. Pei. The main pyramid is accompanied by three smaller ones, and like all great architecture it is both an artistic statement and an aesthetic solution to various practical problems. The tip of the main pyramid in the Cours Napoleon is like the tip of an iceberg, reminding visitors that the Louvre building is only a tiny part of the

OPPOSITE *While many people pay only brief visits to the Louvre to see its most famous art works, the museum houses tens of thousands of items. Every one would reward more thoughtful study*

BELOW *The famous glass pyramid outside the Louvre can be looked at from many angles, inside and out, and provides a range of ever-changing views*

Louvre collection, and that the collection on display is only a small portion of the whole. But Pei's pyramid also enabled the development of a new underground entrance to the Louvre, creating new space and bringing light into it through the reflections and refractions of the glass diamonds used in its construction. The glass and steel is also an echo of more traditional Paris building design, from the late 19th century.

If the outside of the Louvre is both inspiring and impressive, the inside can be almost overwhelming. Even a full day's visit cannot begin to do it justice. Coach parties hurry through, following guides whose task it is to pick out the highlights for them. These naturally include Leonardo da Vinci's *Mona Lisa*, and it sometimes seems as if people are happy to travel half-way round the world for just a brief glimpse of this one small and subtle painting. Géricault's *Raft of the Medusa* is another highlight but it could hardly be more different, being a dramatic canvas delivered on an epic scale.

Of the sculptures, the *Venus de Milo* and the *Winged Victory of Samothrace* both stand out, while Donatello's *Madonna and Child* and *Slaves* by Michelangelo are among the gems of the Italian Sculpture collection. There is a fine collection of Dutch paintings, including works by Rembrandt, Frans Hals and Vermeer, whose painting *The Lacemaker* is considered to be his major masterpiece.

The Louvre's collection stretches around the world, with beautiful displays of Oriental and Islamic art, and back into antiquity too, to the ancient Greeks and the Egyptians. Its Egyptian collection is the largest to be found outside Egypt itself, with about 5,000 items on display out of a total of some 55,000 that are held. These range from impressive large statues and parts of statues, tombs and sphinxes, and numerous mummies, to more evocative everyday items like children's toys, sandals, mirrors and cosmetics, which have miraculously survived from 5,000 years ago. The world should treasure the treasures of the Louvre.

PREVIOUS PAGES *Old and new co-exist at the Louvre, as they do in many parts of Paris, a city that is forever re-inventing itself while seeming to remain unchanged*

ABOVE *The display of some 35,000 items is spread across three wings and several floors and covers some of the world's greatest civilizations from about 7,000BC up to 1848*

LEFT *Part of the Louvre's sculpture collection is displayed in the glass-roofed Cours Marly, including some winged horses (in the background), which were from the gardens of King Louis XIV at Marly*

L'Opéra

In contrast to the modern Opéra Bastille (see pages 56-57), Paris's original Opera House, the Opéra Palais Garnier, is testament to the wealth of the Second Empire in the late 19th century. Commissioned by Napoleon III and designed by Charles Garnier, when it opened in 1875 it was the largest theatre in the world. To call it a Palace was no exaggeration, as it is more splendid and lavish than many a royal household and took 15 years to complete from design to opening night.

While not huge by modern standards, with seating for just 2,200 people, the stage can find room for 450 performers and its red and gold décor, its five tiers of boxes and enormous crystal chandeliers, make a clear statement that this is one of the world's greatest opera

houses. Not content to rest on its Second Empire laurels, the artist Marc Chagall was commissioned in 1964 to paint the auditorium's domed ceiling, and he produced a series of murals inspired by nine different operas.

Many visitors are happy to settle for just a glimpse into this operatic palace, on one of the guided tours or simply by stepping inside to the box office, which also gives a view of the Grand Staircase with its wide white marble stairs and the chandeliers above. Today it is used mainly for ballet performances, with operas staged at the newer Opéra Bastille. The Garnier's legacy, though, is kept in the small library/museum, which has changing exhibitions and holds over 100,000 drawings, paintings, photographs and other items from the building's distinguished history.

L'Orangerie

ABOVE *Once a winter home for citrus trees, the Musée de l'Orangerie is now more famous as a home for water lilies*

What was once a humble greenhouse, built in 1852 as a winter home for orange trees from the Jardin des Tuileries in which it stands, l'Orangerie today houses one of Paris's many small but fine art collections. The highlight is the stunning display of eight of Monet's huge impressionistic canvases of waterlilies, painted in about 1914 at his home in Giverney. They are displayed on their own in the basement of the building, and a recent lengthy restoration project ensures they are shown in a manner that had the artist's personal approval.

Les Nymphéas, to give the series of paintings their French name, have been at l'Orangerie since 1927, and in 1984 they were joined by the fine Walter-Guillaume collection, comprising more Impressionist paintings and works from the early 20th century (which is when l'Orangerie became an art gallery).

The Walter-Guillaume collection includes another Monet, his painting of Argenteuil, as well as works by Renoir, Picasso, Rousseau, Matisse, Sisley, Utrillo, Modigliani and no fewer than 14 works by Cézanne. These include portraits of his wife and his son, while some of Renoir's studies of his children are beautifully tender and touching. There are also some Renoir nude studies, and several by Picasso too. Picasso's paintings of *The Embrace* and *Les Adolescents* are also on display here, but Monet's studies of the changing colours and shapes of the waterlilies in his garden are worth the visit alone.

LEFT *Several of Monet's vast canvases are housed in a special room that was approved by the artist and which surrounds the viewer with water, with nature, with light and with Monet's artistic vision*

Palais-Royal

The Palais-Royal, with its gardens and sculptures, is easily overlooked, even though it is right in the heart of Paris. It is something not to be missed, though, as the gardens can provide some much-needed peace from the city's busy streets, and there are also some striking modern sculptures by way of contrast to the surrounding architecture.

Paris seems to have no shortage of royal palaces, but this particular complex was originally the Palais-Cardinal. It was built in 1632 by Cardinal Richelieu, the advisor to King Louis XIII, who wanted a home near to the Louvre. On the Cardinal's death in 1642 he left the building to the king, who was to die the following year. It then became a royal residence when the regent, Anne of Austria, moved in with her son, Louis XIV, and it was she who gave it the name of the Palais-Royal.

In the 18th century the various arcades and apartments that surround the gardens were added, and it was here in the gardens soon after this, in 1789, that Camille Desmoulins delivered a speech that initiated the storming of the Bastille. Today the buildings contain mainly government offices.

At the southern corner of the Palais-Royal once stood the Théâtre du Petit Cardinal, where the actor-writer Molière (real name Jean-Baptiste Poquelin, 1622-73) would often perform with his troupe. It was on the stage of the theatre that Molière fell ill during a performance of, ironically, his own work *Le Malade Imaginaire* (The Hypochondriac). He died a few hours later.

The apartments that were added in the 18th century have since housed some illustrious tenants, including the artist and author Jean Cocteau, and the writer Colette, who would often sit gazing out of her window at the people passing by underneath. Today she would see Parisians reading their newspapers, children running round the modern sculptures, and a handful of visitors lucky enough to have stumbled into this little retreat.

BELOW: *The one-time Royal Palace now houses the French Ministry of Culture*

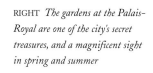

RIGHT *The gardens at the Palais-Royal are one of the city's secret treasures, and a magnificent sight in spring and summer*

Marais & the Bastille

Stretching east from the city centre, the Marais district leads into the Bastille quarter. It has a relaxed air with some beautiful old mansions, several museums including the Picasso Museum, and one of the nicest squares in the city, the Place des Vosges.

The Marais' main street, the rue St-Antoine, is one of many that lead into the busy place de la Bastille, site of the infamous Bastille prison and one of the major Paris squares (see pages 58-59). East from here is the Bastille district, which merges into Faubourg St-Antoine. This has until recently been a much more rough and ready area, known mainly for its furniture workshops. It is slowly becoming more gentrified, and is a fascinating part of the city to wander around, with its cobbled side streets where the workshops can still be found.

But it is the Marais that attracts far more visitors, and this too was once as run down as the Bastille quarter. Originally it was just a stretch of marshland on the edge of the city proper, and that's where the name comes from, *marais* being a marsh. It was gradually settled, and by the 17th century it had become a desirable part of the city, which is why there are so many elegant mansions lining its streets, several of which now house museums. Sadly these became neglected and by the middle of the 20th century the Marais was run down. In 1962 French Culture Minister André Malraux initiated a restoration project which transformed the Marais into the delightful area we see today.

The drama of the Bastille prison's history is captured in these colourful tiles decorating the platforms of the Bastille Métro station

47

Archives Nationales

If the word 'archives' produces a mental picture of rows of shelves of dusty, crumbling documents of interest to only a handful of historians, the French National Archives would change that image totally. They contain, just by way of example, the originals of such documents as the will of Napoleon, the Declaration of Human Rights, letters written by Joan of Arc and Charlemagne, Marie-Antoinette's last communication before she was taken to the guillotine and the diary that King Louis XVI kept while the French Revolution was happening around him. His entry for 14 July 1789, the day of the Storming of the Bastille, was simply '*Rien*' ('Nothing').

Currently a visitor would need a good knowledge of French to appreciate fully the historical treasures that are on display, although there are plans to broaden the interpretations available of the documents, and to extend the scope of the Archives into a museum devoted to the history of France. No knowledge of French is needed, however, to admire the grand building in which the National Archives are kept, the Hôtel de Soubise.

The hôtel – and the word in French means a house not necessarily a hotel – was built as a private dwelling for the Princess de Soubise between 1705 and 1712. There was already a mansion standing here, which dated back to the 14th century, and the Gothic gateway that was built in 1380 still stands. Work on the house continued into the 18th century, and it was considered to be the grandest house in Paris at the time. It's possible to visit the Prince's apartments on the ground floor, then climb a 19th-century staircase to the Princess's Apartments above, giving a glimpse of the grandeur in which the family lived.

BELOW *This sumptuous chamber is one of many fine rooms contained in the Hôtel Soubise, which is one of two Marais mansions that house the French National Archives. The Soubise was built in 1705 for the wealthy François de Rohan-Soubise*

RIGHT *The adjacent Hôtel de Rohan was also built in 1705 for François's son, Cardinal Rohan*

Hôtel de Ville

The present City Hall, which the Mayor of Paris calls home, was built from 1874-84 as a replica of the previous building, which was burned down in the Communard uprising of 1871. The history of the City Hall goes back much further, though, back to 1264, when King Louis IX created the first city authority. He permitted the merchants of Paris to appoint the city's first magistrates in order to govern the city. They met in various places until a permanent home for the expanding city council was found here at the eastern end of the rue de Rivoli, in a mansion called the Maison du Dauphin in the place de Grève.

In the way of governing bodies everywhere, it was decided that a new home was needed more befitting their status, and the Maison du Dauphin was replaced by the grand and imposing – and expensive – Hôtel de Ville.

Work began in 1532 but stopped for various reasons at the second floor, and the building was not finished until 1628. All along the front and roof stand 136 statues of important historical figures.

Today the Hôtel de Ville and the pleasant pedestrian square in front of it are fondly regarded by Parisians. One important reason for this is that in 1944 it formed the base for the French Resistance movement against the invading German armies, and the Resistance were able to hold out for five days against the Nazi forces, until reinforcements came to relieve them.

After its tumultuous history, the square today makes a relaxing place, with fountains at either end helping to drown the noise of the city centre traffic, and there is plenty about the City Hall to look at and admire.

OPPOSITE *Ships once moored where the Hôtel de Ville stands, when the River Seine was much wider. It was later a place for public executions*

BELOW CENTRE *The walls and roof of the City Hall support 136 different statues of important people in the history of France*

BELOW *The early evening sunlight illuminates the fine details on the façade, and the clock of the Paris Hôtel de Ville*

Musée Carnavalet

The Carnavalet Museum not only tells the history of the city of Paris, it plays a part in it itself. It is one of the oldest museums in the city, having been opened in 1880, the brainchild of Baron Haussmann, the architect who reshaped the face of Paris in the late 19th century and so helped create the city that the world admires today. In order to create that city, though, Haussmann also had to demolish many 17th-century mansions in order to widen the boulevards, and some of the finest interiors of those mansions were saved and have been reconstructed here in the Musée Carnavalet.

The museum now comprises two adjoining buildings, but the main one, the Hôtel Carnavalet, was built in the 1540s for the president of the Paris parliament, Jacques de Ligneris. In 1660 the acclaimed architect François Mansart added a new wing, and shortly after that one of the house's most distinguished residents, wit and writer Madame de Sévigné (1626-96) moved in. After being opened as a

BELOW The Musée Carnavalet covers all aspects of the history of Paris, from the lives of kings and queens to its commerce, such as this reconstructed art nouveau shop front

museum in 1880, the next major date in its development was the addition of the neighbouring Hôtel Le Peletier de St-Fargeau, with which the museum now seamlessly links through a first-floor gallery.

The collection ranges from prehistoric to early 20th century, and tells the story of Paris not by conventional chronological means but more haphazardly, in an episodic and more impressionistic fashion. It is a place for wandering along corridors, ascending vast marble staircases and taking diversions into galleries and rooms that may or may not lead to somewhere else. Along the way can be found items like a set of keys to the Bastille prison, the furniture used by the royal family while imprisoned in the Conciergerie during the Revolution, Napoleon Bonaparte's picnic basket (containing 110 pieces of crockery and cutlery) and a large and fascinating collection of paintings of Paris, giving a vivid picture of how the city has looked and changed over the centuries.

ABOVE *The two adjoining buildings that house the Musée Carnavalet, with their gardens, galleries and ivy-clad arcades, are as much a part of the city's history as the museum's contents*

FAR LEFT *The interior of the grand store of Fouquet's, shown opposite, has also been preserved in the Musée Carnavalet*

LEFT *Statues guard staircases in this warren of history and mystery*

53

Musée Picasso

We have taxes to thank for the very existence of this museum, and for the mansion that contains it. It opened in 1985, 12 years after the death of Pablo Picasso (1881-1973), and houses most of the work that the artist's heirs gave to the state in order to settle his death duties. So large was the tax bill that the state received one-quarter of Picasso's collection, which was further added to when Picasso's widow died in 1990. It is a very broad collection from an artist who was immensely skilled in any art form to which he turned, and the collection contains over 200 paintings, over 150 sculptures and ceramics, 16 collages and over 1500 drawings, prints and photographs. As if this weren't enough, the museum also shows Picasso's own personal collection of works by other artists, including Matisse, Renoir, Miró, Braque and Cézanne.

It is usually Picasso's more outrageous and abstract canvases that people remember and associate most closely with his style, but the collection here in the Marais will show anyone just what a hugely talented and varied artist he was. The sketches show that he was a brilliant draughtsman, and there are tender portraits of women and children as well as bold nudes. Some of his ceramics show the whimsical side to his nature, too.

The museum is housed in the Hôtel Salé, or Salty House, built in the 17th century to house a salt-tax collector. It changed hands several times, and was bought by the city of Paris in 1962. In 1976 work began on getting it ready to become the Picasso Museum, and while the financial wranglings over the tax due on the artist's estate went on, work continued, and Diego Giacometti was commissioned to produce the chandeliers and some of the furniture.

In this building, one artist pays tribute to another – while Picasso pays his tribute to the taxman.

BELOW *All styles and periods of Picasso's work are displayed at the Musée Picasso in the Marais, including the wonderful* Femmes à Leur Toilette *(1938)*

OPPOSITE *Some paintings require more thought than others*

Opéra Bastille

The storming of the Bastille prison took place on 14 July 1789, and 200 years later to the day, the largest opera house in the world, the Opéra National de Paris Bastille, was opened at the far side of the place de la Bastille. It had quite a stormy opening, as critics and audiences alike lamented the poor sound quality compared to the venerable old Opéra Garnier (see pages 40-41). The starkly

modern style of the building also came in for criticism, not helped by the fact that there were teething troubles such as tiles dropping off the façade.

However, the acoustical and other problems were dealt with and the quality of the sound in the auditorium today is said to be as good as anywhere. People have also got used to the modern design of the building, which can look

dramatic lit up at night, but it has never been quite as successful as some other recent additions, such as the Pompidou Centre see pages 26-29) or Pei's pyramid outside the Louvre (see pages 34-39).

The Opéra was designed by a Uruguayan-born Canadian, Carlos Ott, and was chosen from 744 entries. The grey marble and glass exterior can give dramatic reflections of the area around, while inside the auditorium the use of glass, wood and granite gives an equally striking

but more pleasing look. The steeply sloping space seats 2,700 people, and there are several studios and rehearsal rooms for the artists, two restaurants and large costume and scenery stores. Backstage tours are popular, and usually provide a look at the ingenious stage system whereby any of six separate platforms can be moved into place to save the need to change scenery behind the stage. Paris now has two world-class opera houses, the classical and the unapologetically modern.

ABOVE *Depending on the light, the geometric façade of the Opéra Bastille building sometimes reflects its surroundings, and sometimes allows a look within*

Place de la Bastille

The place de la Bastille will be forever associated with the notorious prison that stood on this spot, and which housed such famous prisoners as Voltaire, the Marquis de Sade and the mysterious Man in the Iron Mask, whose identity has never been revealed.

The Bastille was not originally a prison but a bastion guarding the gate that marked the eastern entry into the city of Paris. It was King Charles V who added further towers, thick walls and a wide moat to turn the bastion into a fortress. Later it became the main place for holding political prisoners, with a reputation for being impossible to escape from – though escapes did occur. It also had a fierce reputation for the grimness of its conditions, which was why in July 1789 the Revolutionaries stormed the prison, which was seen as a symbol of repression. This was also the act that effectively launched the French Revolution and overthrew the monarchy.

It was the start of the biggest but not the last French Revolution, and it is later rebellions that are marked by the Colonne de Juillet or July Column. This stands in the centre of the traffic-filled modern place de la Bastille, which was laid out in 1803 as an open space to replace the demolished prison. The July Column marks the events of July 1830, July obviously being a popular month for uprisings in Paris. The revolt of 1830 caused three days of fighting in the streets and the death of 504 people, who are buried beneath the column, which was erected in 1840. Victims of a further revolution in February 1848 are also buried beneath the column, which is 164ft (50m) high and topped by a gold and bronze figure, the Spirit of Liberty.

LEFT *The Colonne de Juillet, the July Column, is a proud but chilling reminder that beneath its circular base lie the interred bodies of 504 people who died here in street-fighting in July 1830*

RIGHT *The bronze-gilt figure of Liberty, which tops the Colonne de Juillet, here seems to hark back to stormier days during the dramatic light and swirling clouds of a solar eclipse*

Place des Vosges

The place des Vosges, at the heart of the Marais, is the oldest square in Paris. Some also think it the most beautiful, and certainly the local residents as well as visitors enjoy its benches and fountains. Children play, old people watch them, lovers hold hands and tourists take photographs. And occasionally perhaps someone spares a thought for King Henri IV, who decided to lay out this square as the then place Royale, which was opened in 1612 by the new king, Louis XIII, as one of the very first examples of town planning in the city of Paris. A statue of Louis stands in the centre of the square.

The name place Royale was given because a royal palace once stood here, but it was torn down in the 16th century by Catherine de Medici after her husband King Henri II was accidentally killed in a tournament here during some marriage celebrations. Her tragic loss was undoubtedly the future's gain. The change from place Royale to place des Vosges came about in 1800, when the French department of Vosges became the first to pay off its share of liabilities for the Revolutionary Wars, and was rewarded by having this elegant square named in its honour.

Over the years the place des Vosges has had some distinguished residents, indicating its desirability as a Paris address. These have included Cardinal Richelieu, Madame de Sévigné, Victor Hugo, Richard Rogers and Francis Bacon. They have all lived in the 36 houses which surround the square, nine on each side, with distinctive red-brick and stone frontages, steeply sloping tiled roofs, and graceful shady arcades running around the square. The ground floors now contain galleries, cafés, shops and restaurants catering to the many visitors, but the square has lost none of its elegance.

ABOVE *The attractive arcades that surround the elegant place des Vosges provide shelter from sun and rain, and a popular spot to enjoy a meal or a drink*

RIGHT AND OPPOSITE *For almost 400 years the windows of the buildings around the place des Vosges have looked down on the comings and goings of generation after generation, of young and old, residents and visitors, rich and poor, as they go about their business*

St-Germain & the Left Bank

To many people – Parisians and visitors – the Left Bank is Paris. It's the Paris of pleasure. It's the Paris of cafés and jazz, of restaurants and Bohemians, of students, immigrants, writers, artists, and philosophers too. It has gardens and museums, one of the oldest churches in Paris and some of the most impressive modern architecture in the Institute du Monde Arabe and the Bibliothèque Nationale de France.

St-Germain and the boulevard St-Germain are probably the best-known names, but there's the Latin Quarter too, and the Left Bank extends east and west and encompasses the university of the Sorbonne, the Panthéon, where some of France's more notable citizens are laid to rest, and the Jardin du Luxembourg, one of the city's most popular parks.

These streets were familiar to visitors like Ernest Hemingway, Scott Fitzgerald, James Joyce and Pablo Picasso, and to French intellectuals such as Jean-Paul Sartre and Simone de Beauvoir. They worked, played and held court in some of the area's famous cafés, which are as busy today as they ever were – names like the Café de Flore, Les Deux Magots and the Brasserie Lipp.

The district is as alive as it ever was, with some of the city's top restaurants and stylish boutique hotels, with lively food shops and street markets like the one on the rue de Buci, which show that people do still live, work and shop in this very Parisian Faubourg.

Parisians love their daily bread, and none more so than the revered name of Poilâne, whose fabulous shop display shows just how sumptuous this staple food can become

Bibliothèque Nationale de France – François Mitterand

Writers and literature have always been at the heart of this part of Paris, and are of course revered throughout France. The French treat novelists with the same high regard they give to intellectuals and philosophers, and libraries are seen as an essential part of the urban landscape. That doesn't mean they need to be dull, as the example of the library at the Pompidou Centre shows, and also here at the home of the National Library.

Work began on the building in 1990, and it is named after President Mitterand, as it was one of the *grands projets* that he initiated during his time as President. The four L-shaped towers represent books standing upright and open, and they provide storage space for 15 million volumes. The National Collection of France is rivalled in Europe only by the British Library in London, and dates back to the 15th century. It had various temporary homes as it constantly expanded, finally settling

in the 17th century at the first Bibliothèque Nationale building on rue de Richelieu, north of the Palais-Royal.

Naturally it continued to expand at ever-greater speeds. In 1793 an act was passed that required the deposit of one copy of every book, newspaper, magazine or other publication at the National Library, which eventually necessitated the creation of a new building and the transfer of the collection between 1996 and 1998.

The library is open to everyone, and there are guided tours designed to show off some of the building's special features. There are concealed sunken gardens, exhibition halls, a café, a bookshop and reading rooms. Anyone can acquire a day ticket, which will give them access to the several hundred thousand volumes that in the open collection, as well as CDs, videos and DVDs, while anyone is possession of a special reader's ticket can consult a further 400,000 books.

RIGHT *France's National Library sometimes looks like rows of closed books on a shelf*

FAR RIGHT *Sometimes the library looks like books standing open in a perfect and playful blend of form and function*

Boulevard St-Germain

If the Left Bank is archetypal Paris, the boulevard St-Germain is archetypal Left Bank. It's the backbone of the district, the main street that runs for about 2 miles (3km) through the Latin Quarter and St-Germain districts, and along it are some of the cafés that have made this area famous, like the Café Flore and, opposite it, Les Deux Magots.

At the Deux Magots in times gone by you might have sat at the next table to artists and writers such as Oscar Wilde, Ernest Hemingway, Paul Verlaine or Pablo Picasso. It was here that Picasso met his muse, Dora Maar, in 1937, and the café features in Hemingway's memoirs of Paris, *A Moveable Feast*, and in his novel *The Sun Also Rises*. The art-deco Café Flore was more popular with the Left Bank intellectuals like Jean-Paul Sartre and Simone de Beauvoir, who virtually set up office here, and Albert Camus. The nearby Brasserie Lipp, with its art-nouveau interior, has always been a favourite of politicians as well as journalists and newspaper editors. Presidents including Mitterand, Pompidou and de Gaulle have all dined there.

Set back from the boulevard on place St-Germain-des-Prés is the church of the same name, which is possibly the oldest in Paris. It was built in 1163 but was outside the city walls, so the church of St-Julien-le-Pauvre, which was built two years later but within the city walls, makes claim to being the oldest in the city. One of St-Germain's 12th-century towers still stands, and inside it is one of the oldest belfries in France, but much of the rest of the church was restored in the 19th century. The history of the area is indicated by the fact that there was a church here as far back as 542, built to house what was said to be a piece of the Holy Cross that had been brought back from Spain a few years earlier.

BELOW AND RIGHT *The Café de Flore is just one of several cafés on and around the boulevard St-Germain where artists have met writers and philosophers, and where politicians have met journalists – not just for decades but for centuries*

LEFT *Paris has always been a multi-cultural city and the presence of its strong Arabic community is acknowledged here in the Institute du Monde Arabe, with its beautifully inventive windows*

Institute du Monde Arabe

The striking design of the Institute of the Arab World shows how Paris can so easily incorporate a building that blends ancient and modern Islamic style into its own architectural mix of the new and the old. The building was opened in 1987 but the idea goes back to 1974, when France met with 19 Arab countries and together they decided to create this Institute here in the heart of Paris. Designer Jean Nouvel is the main creative brain behind this unusual building.

The famous south face of the building is made up of 240 identical metal screens, whose design is based on the traditional Islamic wooden screens known as *moucharabiehs*. But the ones on the Institute incorporate 1,600 light-sensitive devices which adjust to the sunlight like the iris of an eye or the lens of a camera, controlling the amount of light that is permitted to enter the building. They adjust every hour but can also be changed manually, for days when there are sudden dramatic changes in the light. To see the whole side of the building adjust itself to the light is quite something.

Among the other high-tech creations that sit side-by-side with traditional features like a Moorish courtyard is the high-speed transparent lift. This takes visitors up to the museum and various exhibitions that spread across several floors of the Institute. It also houses a cinema, theatre, an excellent restaurant, cafés, research facilities and a library of over 50,000 books, with nine floors above ground and a further two floors below.

Taking the lifts to the top floor is an experience in itself, and at the top a terrace with its own Moorish tea room provides views across the River Seine to the solid splendour of Nôtre-Dame, a reminder of the contrasting architectural face of Paris, and the multi-faith nature of this modern European city.

OPPOSITE *The windows of the Institute also reflect the Moorish customs of secret screens, of harems, of private courtyards, where people can observe without being observed*

Jardin du Luxembourg

One of the best and most popular parks in Paris provides a breath of fresh air away from the busy Left Bank streets. It owes its existence to Marie de Médici, widow of King Henri IV, and its name to Duke François of Luxembourg. Marie was bored with life in the Louvre – after all, having only one royal palace can get a bit dull – so she bought some land from Duke François and commissioned architect Salomon de Brosse to produce a palace and gardens that would remind her of her native Florence. It was to be designed in the style of her birthplace, the Pitti Palace, and would give her a rural retreat where she could escape from the busy Louvre.

This was in 1615 and the work took about 10 years to complete, but soon afterwards Marie was exiled by Cardinal Richelieu and so was not able to enjoy the palace and gardens for very long. In those days the gardens were much bigger, but a large area was lost during Baron Haussmann's redesign of Paris during the mid-19th century. Nevertheless, some 60 acres (24 hectares) still remain, containing among many other things a bandstand, carousel, fountains, children's play areas and pony rides, cafés, a pond and 80 statues, as well as people playing boules or chess, throwing frisbees and flying kites, playing tennis, sailing boats, visiting the bee-keeping school or enjoying the puppet show at the marionette theatre.

Some famous names have also enjoyed these activities, although perhaps Jean-Paul Sartre did not throw a frisbee. The writer Ernest Hemingway in his book about Paris, *A Moveable Feast*, claims to have caught pigeons in the gardens in order to eat when he was new to the city and penniless. Other names are commemorated in stone, as among the garden's statues you might find a bust of Beethoven, carvings of Stendhal and George Sand, and monuments to Delacroix and Watteau. One of the two

fountains in the gardens also commemorates their instigator, Marie. The impressive Fontaine Médici was built by Salomon de Brosse for Marie in the style of an Italian grotto.

Another familiar figure is that of the Statue of Liberty, as the Jardin Anglais (English Garden) contains a copy of Bartholdi's sculpture that was given to the United States in 1885. The one in the garden was installed in 1906. Music lovers should time their visit to coincide with one of the summer afternoon concerts held in the bandstand, while families can enjoy puppet shows at the Théâtre des Marionnettes on weekend mornings and afternoons, and on Wednesday afternoons too. It's a chance to see the French version of Punch and Judy, the *Guignols*, which originated in the southern city of Lyons, but the archetypal characters of Beaujolais-swilling drunks and their foolish friends are familiar all over France.

The palace itself has had a very chequered and interesting history. It was originally known as the Palais Médici, but became the Palais d'Orléans when it passed to Marie's second son Gaston, the Duc d'Orléans. During the Revolution it was put to use as a prison, and then took its turn as the seat of government. It became the Palais du Consulat, and then the Palais du Senat. It was the home of the French Senate from 1852 until 1940, and then during World War II it became the headquarters of the German Luftwaffe. It was handed back to the Senate in 1958, which is still based there today, making the palace off-limits to visitors.

ABOVE *The Jardin du Luxembourg is a setting where mankind's creative work has a backdrop of nature's beauty through its changing seasons*

OPPOSITE *In places the Luxembourg Gardens provide a background of sensuous statues, reflecting the romances and tragedies that have been played out here over the years – both those we know about and those that remain secret*

LEFT *Sometimes, of course, all a man desires is a seat in the morning sun and the simple pleasure of feeding the birds*

Musée Cluny

The Musée National du Moyen Âge-Thermes de Cluny, or Musée Cluny for short, is not the best known of Paris's museums but it has a unique collection of medieval items set in one of Paris's oldest mansions. The Hôtel de Cluny is itself a medieval masterpiece, built at the end of the 15th century for wealthy Benedictine monks from Cluny in Burgundy so that they would have a base near the capital. For a time it was home to Mary Tudor, the sister of King Henry VIII of England, who was married to King Louis XII of France but widowed after only three months. The mansion was bought by the art collector Alexandre du Sommerard in the early 19th century and it is his wonderful collection that forms the core of the museum's exhibits today.

There are about 23,000 items on display, which gives some indication of just how much is packed into this small but warren-like building. At times it can seem like wandering round some private Gothic castle, never quite sure what is at the end of the next corridor. The highlight of the museum's collection is the display of six 15th-century Dutch tapestries woven from wool and silk and known collectively as *La Dame à la Licorne* (*The Lady and the Unicorn*).

The museum contains some of the heads that were hacked off the statues on the west front of Nôtre-Dame (see pages 18-21) by Revolutionaries who mistakenly believed them to represent French kings. They were in fact Biblical figures, created in the 13th century, and lost to the world until they were found in a bank vault in 1977.

The second part of the museum's name refers to the Gallo-Roman baths that were on this site in the 2nd century AD and the remains of which can still be seen.

Muséum National d'Histoire Naturelle

France's National Museum of Natural History occupies several galleries within the Jardin des Plantes, but the main attraction is the innovative Grand Galerie de l'Évolution. It's a modern display in an old building, which adds to its appeal. The glass-roofed building opened in 1889 as the Zoological Gallery, but it was neglected over the years and finally closed in 1965. The replacement Grand Galerie was one of President Mitterand's *grands projets* and it opened in 1994 to great acclaim.

BELOW *The wonderful Dinosaur Pavilion in Paris's National Museum of Natural History*

The gallery tells the story of evolution, and the central spectacle on the ground floor is a display of animals seemingly marching across the African savannah. It's an impressive sight, and a brilliantly clever way of using the collection of stuffed creatures to good effect. They walk beneath the central atrium, while suspended above them is the huge skeleton of a whale, with sound effects piped around the gallery significantly adding to the drama.

Other galleries run around the sides of the building, both illustrating and questioning other aspects of the evolution of life on earth, including man's ability to destroy the planet. Down below, in the basement, the wonders of the oceans are explored.

Live animals can be observed at the Ménagerie, also in the Jardin des Plantes, where over 1,100 mammals, birds and reptiles are housed and cared for, in a collection that dates back to 1794. It was formed after the French Revolution, mainly from animals that had been held in the royal collection at Versailles, and supplemented with others taken from street entertainers. The Ménagerie – the oldest in France – also incorporates a Microzoo of spiders and insects that can be examined under microscopes by those not too squeamish about these smallest of creatures from the Natural History collection.

ABOVE *Outside the Museum of Natural History some rather unnatural creatures can also be found, like this animated fire-breathing dragon*

Musée d'Orsay

So rich are the art collections held in Paris that three museums are needed to house the treasures. Covering the short but immensely productive period from the mid-19th century to the early 20th century, and sandwiched between the classical collection at the Louvre and the modern collection at the Pompidou Centre, stands the magnificent Musée d'Orsay.

Even though it covers only the short period from 1848 to 1914, the Musée d'Orsay is easily the equal of the other two collections and attracts just as many visitors. In fact so popular are its star exhibits by the Impressionists that at

busy periods it can be as crowded in front of the Van Goghs as it is in front of the *Mona Lisa* at the Louvre. Many visitors, though, come to *see* the paintings rather than *look* at them, and therefore the crowds can move on quite quickly.

A visit to the Musée d'Orsay provides full proof that Paris really knows how to do museums. The visit is an experience in itself, regardless of the countless priceless art works on display. The building is a former railway station, the Gare d'Orsay, that was built in 1900 to help bring visitors to that year's Paris Exposition. The station closed in 1939, however, and was disused for many years apart from occasions like the 1962 filming there by Orson

Welles of Kafka's *The Trial*. There were plans to knock it down in the 1970s, but it earned a reprieve in 1977 when the decision was taken to turn it into this impressive modern art museum, which was opened in December 1986 by the French President, François Mitterand.

The building's origins are still evident, with the original station clock telling the time in the café while the excellent restaurant retains the turn-of-the-century décor of the station hotel. The hotel's ballroom has also been conserved, with its mirrors and grand chandeliers, and can be found at the end of the middle level of the museum.

But the museum today is filled with space and light rather than noise and steam, and houses some of the most

valuable and best-loved paintings in the world, by the Impressionists and Post-Impressionists. These are the most famous exhibits, though they form only about one-third of the overall collection, which includes sculpture, photographs and furniture, as well as examples from the many other art movements that were prevalent in the late 19th and early 20th centuries.

Famous names like Renoir, Monet, Toulouse-Lautrec, Manet, Cézanne, Dégas and Rodin are among the star attractions, but the breadth of the collection is enormous, from the elegant furniture of Glasgow's Charles Rennie Mackintosh to the sculpture of Rodin's muse and lover, Camille Claudel. There's also a bust of Claudel among the works by Rodin on display, which include his unforgettable study of Balzac.

One name stands above all others, though, and a chance to view his work brings admirers from all over the globe: Vincent Van Gogh. The bold blues of his *Bedroom at Arles* (*La Chambre à Arles*) and his haunting 1889 self-portrait (one of the last he ever did, the year before his suicide) are among the masterpieces here. Among the other works by Van Gogh that are held at the Musée d'Orsay are *The Siesta, The Portrait of Dr Paul Gachet* and *The Church at Auvers-sur-Oise*.

Another attraction is the work of Dégas, in particular his studies of dancers whether in paint, pastel or as delicate

ABOVE *The delicate subtle-toned paintings and sculptures of dancers by Dégas are among the museum's most admired works*

RIGHT *Renoir is also well represented, with paintings such as* Moulin de la Galette

OPPOSITE *The museum's origins as a train station are still evident, with its glass façade helping to bring light into the huge space*

sculptures. The beautiful bronze *Young Dancer of Fourteen* is here, as is Dégas' painting of *The Dancing Class* and in contrast the very different study showing the grim reality of *The Absinthe Drinkers*.

One unmissable work is the controversial 1863 canvas by Manet, *Le Déjeuner sur l'Herbe*, which caused a major scandal with its depiction of a nude woman dining at a picnic surrounded by gentlemen in suits. Equally shocking was his 1865 portrait of a naked courtesan, *Olympia*, and one of the aspects of a visit to the Musée d'Orsay is seeing a world-famous work almost at every turn. One of the best known and best liked paintings of the Impressionist era is Renoir's *Dancing at the Moulin de la Galette*. Renoir lived in Montmartre, as did many other artists, and he was a regular visitor to the Galette. Toulouse-Lautrec's *Jane Avril Dancing* is probably the most familiar of his several works on show here.

Toulouse-Lautrec, Van Gogh and Henri Matisse are just three of the Post-Impressionists whose works are well represented in the museum, while other artistic movements with substantial collections include the Nabis (Pierre Bonnard, for example), the Romantics, including Delacroix, the Symbolists including Klimt, Munch and Whistler (featuring the famous painting of his mother) and the School of Pont-Aven, centred around Paul

BELOW *An up-close look at the Musée d'Orsay's clock reveals that it is a work of art in itself*

RIGHT *The exterior gives no indication that the building contains one of the world's greatest art collections*

Gauguin. Gauguin features strongly at the Musée d'Orsay, both from his time in France and in the South Seas, with several Tahitian paintings on show.

Representing the decorative arts, as well as examples of the work of Glasgow's Art Nouveau designer Charles Rennie Mackintosh there are also some superb examples of jewellery and glass bottles by Lalique. The photography archive contains over 10,000 photographs including some by Dégas, Pierre Bonnard, Atget, Lewis Carroll, George Bernard Shaw and the leading early female photographer, Julia Margaret Cameron.

Like the Louvre on the Right Bank, some of the best views of the Musée d'Orsay are to be had from across the river, where its railway station origins can be seen, and the vast scale of the building gives some hint of the enormous range of treasures to be found inside.

Panthéon

Some of the greatest French men and women who have ever lived are buried here at the Panthéon, a rare honour granted to only a few of the country's most notable citizens. People like Voltaire, Madame Curie, Louis Braille, and Victor Hugo have been interred here.

It is much more than merely a final resting place for the great and the good, though. It is an impressive building in its own right, having been commissioned by King Louis XV as a basilica dedicated to the patron saint of Paris, St Geneviève, as thanks for his recovery from a serious case of gout. The king himself laid the foundation stone in 1764, but the building, which was partly inspired by the Pantheon in Rome, was not completed until 1790. Its function as a basilica was short-lived, as a year later its windows were bricked up by Revolutionaries, who turned it into a secular building to honour worthy citizens.

One of the Panthéon's most notable features is the dome, from which the scientist Foucault hung a pendulum in 1851, noting the way that the pendulum moved, showing that its motion was caused by the constant spinning of the earth on its axis.

It is down below ground, in the shadowy crypt, that the tombs of the notable citizens can be found. People like Louis Braille, who invented the Braille language for blind people, are honoured here, along with Marie and Pierre Curie. Philosophers, physicists and chemists including Voltaire, Rousseau and Diderot are buried here, and many notable writers too, such as Victor Hugo and André Malraux. Many are moved to the Panthéon some time after their death, as was the case with Émile Zola and, most recently, Alexandre Dumas. The author of *The Three Musketeers* and many other popular novels was re-buried in the Panthéon on 29 November 2002.

St-Sulpice

The monumental church of St-Sulpice was founded in 1646 by the abbey of St-Germain-des-Prés, which employed six architects over the period of 134 years that it took to build the church. The long time span was due to the scale of the venture, financial problems, and a lightning strike which halted work for a time. It's truer to say that work was halted in 1780 rather than finished, as the south tower is still incomplete and is 16ft (5m) shorter than the north tower.

As the church neared its completion in 1776, an organ was designed for it that used 6,588 pipes and was therefore one of the largest and most powerful in the world. It is still in use for organ recitals, something not to be missed if the opportunity arises. St-Sulpice stands on the zero meridian, indicated by a bronze strip which runs from the north to the south transept. At noon on the winter solstice the light

of the sun is reflected directly onto a white marble obelisk, at noon on the summer solstice the light hits a marble plaque in the south transept, and on the spring and autumn solstices the light illuminates a bronze table in the south transept.

The Chapelle des Anges includes some fascinating murals by Eugène Delacroix, made late in the artist's life: *Jacob Wrestling with the Angel, Heliodorus Chased from the Temple* and *St Michael Vanquishing the Devil*. Also remarkable are the two fonts of holy water inside the main door, made from huge shells that were given to King François I by the Venetian Republic. There are also some beautiful 17th-century stained-glass windows, an elaborately carved and gilded pulpit dating back to 1788 and many paintings, frescoes and statues spread around this amazing church.

ABOVE *The north tower of St-Sulpice, on the left of the photo, differs from the south tower on the right. The latter was never completed, and their slightly different styles can easily be seen*

RIGHT *This view over the rooftops of Paris clearly shows why St-Sulpice has been referred to as the Cathedral of the Left Bank*

PAGE 87 *The Marquis de Sade and the poet Baudelaire are among the great and the good who have been christened within the walls of the church of St-Sulpice*

La Sorbonne

The Sorbonne now encompasses four separate Parisian universities: Paris Sorbonne, Sorbonne Nouvelle, Panthéon-Sorbonne and René Descartes. No doubt its founder Robert de Sorbon would be immensely proud of what he created, if he could see it today. Sorbon was the chaplain to King Louis IX (St Louis) and in 1253 he set up a college to house 16 poor theology students. That original college lasted until 1629, when Cardinal Richelieu paid for it to be rebuilt. The Chapelle de la Sorbonne still survives from that era, but the rest of the buildings date from the late 19th century.

The existence of a university in Paris pre-dates even the founding of the Sorbonne, and had its roots at the very start of the 12th century, based at Nôtre-Dame. The Sorbonne became the faculty of theology for the university, but eventually overshadowed the rest of the university because of the importance of religion in French life.

The Sorbonne was always a controversial centre of learning, as it maintained a distance from the state and had its own views on many important matters. It recognized, for example, the English King Henry V as the rightful King of France and refused to support the former-Protestant French King Henri IV; it condemned Joan of Arc, opposed the views of the 18th-century philosophers who were challenging some of the church's thinking, and of course in more recent times it was the students from the Sorbonne who participated in the Student Revolt of 1968 and battled in the streets with the French police.

The university buildings are closed to the public, but it is possible to get a glimpse into the courtyard and the university students are very much in evidence in the cafés and bars that thrive in this area. It is likely that the serious-minded Robert de Sorbon would emphatically not have approved of some of their behaviour today.

ABOVE *By some accounts the Sorbonne dates back to 1208, making it a model for other great universities such as Oxford and Cambridge*

OPPOSITE *Students have been coming to the Sorbonne for well over 750 years, making it one of the oldest universities in Europe. Only Bologna claims to be as old*

LEFT *The Sorbonne's students certainly provide a good trade for the local booksellers and bakers*

Les Invalides & the Tour Eiffel

To the west of the St-Germain and Latin Quarter districts, the area traditionally thought of as the Left Bank, lies Les Invalides. This part of Paris stretches from just west of the Musée d'Orsay, past the National Assembly and the Hôtel des Invalides, where Napoleon lies buried, and reaches all the way to the one unmistakeable symbol of Paris, the Eiffel Tower.

It is a well-to-do part of the city, as you might expect with it containing the lower house of the French Parliament at the National Assembly. There are some expensive restaurants and exclusive food shops, and in the eastern end of the district are some handsome old mansions, several of which have been converted into foreign embassies. There is money here, and it shows. The area was mostly laid out in the 19th century, when the city still had space enough to allow for the building of wide boulevards with trees and open views of the impressive buildings that were being constructed.

It was towards the end of the 19th century when what would become the city's best-known landmark was built. The Eiffel Tower was thought a monstrosity at the time, reviled by many of the people who lived in this exclusive part of the town and had a good view of its construction. Today it's impossible to imagine Paris without it. The best views of all are from the far side of the river, from the Palais de Chaillot, especially when the tower is lit up at night. It is easily the number one view in Paris, outshining even the view from the top.

With a view like this, from the Palais de Chaillot, you could be in no other city in the world but Paris

91

Assemblée Nationale (Palais-Bourbon)

This grand building is home to the French National Assembly, the lower house of the French Parliament – the Senate sits in the Palais du Luxembourg (see pages 70-73). The Palais-Bourbon goes back to 1722-28 when Louise-Françoise Bourbon, the daughter of King Louis XIV, had a mansion built on this site by the River Seine, with the Louvre Palace visible upriver on the other side. The main entrance and the courtyard inside are all that remain of this building, however.

From 1764 to 1789 the Palais-Bourbon was enlarged, just in time for the Revolution to come along, after which the building was claimed for the French nation. Its conversion to political use began in 1798, when it became home briefly to the Council of the Five Hundred. From 1799 until 1808 it was used to house the National Archives, and it was during this period that the north façade was added by Napoleon, in the style of a Greek temple to echo the Hellenistic style of the church of La Madeleine across the river. From 1815 onwards it has been home to one part of the French Parliament, at first called the Chambre des Députés, which later became the Assemblée Nationale.

This lower house has 577 members, who debate in the Chamber of the Palais-Bourbon and have offices nearby. The President of the Assembly enjoys the Hôtel de Lassay as his official residence. This was built in 1724, the same time as the original mansion, and was incorporated into the Palais-Bourbon during the late 18th-century extensions, though only physically connected to it by a gallery added in 1848. The Palais was used as the headquarters of the occupying German forces during World War II. To see the interior of the building, visitors can join one of the guided tours on Saturdays, or hope to gain admission to one of the public debates held during the week – though come early as only the first 10 people in line are admitted.

OPPOSITE *Inside the Assemblée Nationale are artworks, including works by Delacroix, while in the grounds the strolling politicians are subject to a stoney gaze*

BELOW *In the shadow of the Palais-Bourbon there was much fighting when Paris was liberated from the Nazi occupation at the end of World War II. 30,000 volumes from its library were destroyed*

École Militaire

Most visitors are so keen to get to the Eiffel Tower and ascend to the top that they hardly notice the Military School, which stands at the other end of the Champ de Mars. In fact the students and officers at the École Militaire enjoyed a fine view down to the Seine and across the river to the Palais de Chaillot until the tower was built at the end of the 19th century. Today, one of the best views of the Eiffel Tower is from the colonnaded and domed École Militaire, almost rivalling the fine view from the Chaillot gardens.

The school's history goes back to 1751, when it was commissioned by King Louis XV, encouraged by his mistress Madame de Pompadour, who wanted to see a college where impoverished young men could be trained for the military. The building was finished in 1773 and the funding to train the young recruits was found by placing a tax on playing cards and starting a national lottery. Its most famous graduate of all was national hero Napoleon Bonaparte, who began studying at the school in 1784 when he was 15 years old.

It was an appropriate spot for the future leader to learn his skills, as it was on the fields in front of the École Militaire that the invading Romans fought and beat the Parisii tribes in 52BC to move into Paris, and where later the Parisians successfully defended their city against the Vikings. The fields were formally laid out as the Champ de Mars, or the Field of Mars (the Roman God of War), in 1765, during the building of the École for use as its military parade ground. It has subsequently been used at times of national celebration, for horse races and for the Montgolfier brothers to experiment with their hot-air balloons. Today it's a place for anyone to stroll in and enjoy the views of the Eiffel Tower.

LEFT *The Monument de la Paix (Peace Monument) near the École Militaire in the Champs des Mars provides the perfect frame for the Eiffel Tower*

RIGHT *The Military School buildings can really be appreciated when looking down from the Eiffel Tower, with the modern Tour Montparnasse in the background*

Hôtel des Invalides

OPPOSITE *The cannon in the grounds of the Hôtel des Invalides*

OVERLEAF *Hôtel des Invalides is one of the largest military museums in the world, a chronicle of warfare over thousands of years and a vast historical archive*

BELOW RIGHT *Napoleon's tomb is made up of six coffins, one laid inside the other*

BELOW *From the outside, the dome of Les Invalides glints gold in the sun, while inside Napoleon gazes up at this view for all eternity*

Combine a home for invalids, a tomb and an army museum, and many visitors would bypass the area in search of more cheerful attractions. But Les Invalides is one of the most fascinating parts of Paris, a complex that includes some marvellous architecture, one of the finest museums of its kind in the world, and the last resting place of one of the greatest Frenchmen of them all, Napoleon Bonaparte.

It was an earlier great Frenchman, King Louis XIV, who built the main Hôtel des Invalides in 1676 as a hospital for soldiers who had been wounded fighting for their country. At its busiest there were as many as 6,000 soldiers receiving treatment or recuperating here, and there are still a few living there even today. Mainly, though, the buildings have been given over to government offices, but no matter to what use they have been put, the front façade, which is 645ft (196m) long, cannot fail to impress.

It rises to four floors topped by a row of dormer windows standing out from the tiled roof, while above the huge central archway the French flag proudly flies.

Beyond this, and directly in line with it, is a golden dome, marking the Église du Dôme, the Dome Church. And directly below the pinnacle of the dome, below the ground, is the tomb of Napoleon Bonaparte. It's a dramatic resting place for Napoleon, surrounded by other famous French fighting men, including two of his brothers, Joseph and Jérome.

Spread around three wings of the Hôtel, the Musée de l'Armée tells the story of warfare through the ages, and naturally Napoleon features here too. It is an astonishing collection of weapons, armour, maps, paintings and other items, breathtaking in its size and showing some incredible workmanship. Warfare is part of man's story, and it is treated here with a mix of drama and poignancy.

Musée du Quai Branly

This visually startling new museum (opened in 2006) stands literally in the shadow of the Eiffel Tower. Its architect Jean Nouvel, who also designed the Institute du Monde Arabe (see pages 68-69), endeavoured to make positive and creative use of this situation in his designs for the museum, which he wanted to instill with the impression of that shadow. How successful he has been is a matter of some debate, though one remarkable feature is the Living Wall, which contains about 1,500 species of plants growing on it.

Inside, the museum's curators have accumulated state collections of art from the continents of Africa, Asia and Oceania, previously held in important galleries including the Louvre, the former Musée des Arts d'Afrique et d'Océanie and the Musée de l'Homme in the Palais de Chaillot, here displayed together for the first time. The themes of the collections range from African musical instruments to the relationship between humankind and the natural world. The displays are always eye-catching and often dramatic, arranged geographically and using coloured floor tiles to guide the visitor.

Both inside and out, the Musée du Quai Branly is yet another example of how Paris is never content with the mundane when it comes to design.

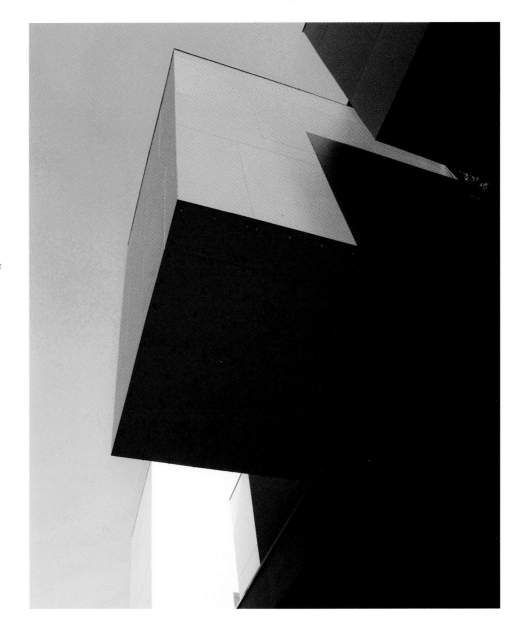

ABOVE *When the museum opened in 2006, architect Jean Nouvel's design created quite a stir*

LEFT *The museum's remarkable collection of anthropological items from around the world has found a stylish new home*

OPPOSITE *The Living Wall covers part of the exterior of the Musée du Quai Branly, a contrast to some of the modern angular designs*

101

RIGHT *The Musée du Quai Branly stands close to the Eiffel Tower, and the architect made use of this in his plans for the building in which he attempted to give a hint of the tower's shadow*

OPPOSITE *The Quai Branly runs along the Left Bank of the Seine, between two contrasting tourist attractions – the Eiffel Tower that soars into the sky, and the Paris sewers, which take visitors beneath the streets*

Musée Rodin

One of the greatest sculptors the world has ever seen, whose works like *The Kiss* and *The Thinker* are known the world over, is well honoured here in the house that was once his home. Auguste Rodin was born in Paris in 1840 and showed an early aptitude for drawing. In 1908 he moved into the rococo Hôtel Biron, built in 1730 by the Duc de Biron, but best known now because Rodin lived and worked there for the final nine years of his life. In 1904 the mansion had been turned into apartments and studios for artists to use, and among those who have lived here are Henri Matisse, Jean Cocteau and the ballet dancer Isadora Duncan. When Rodin moved in four years later, he was allowed to stay and work here rent-free provided he gave his works to the nation when he died. He passed away in 1917, two years later, the Hôtel was turned into the Musée Rodin.

Today the house remains one of the most popular and delightful museums in Paris, all the more so for the knowledge that the artist himself lived and loved here. Works of great genius fill every room, and even outside in the gardens (one of the largest private gardens in the city) you will constantly come across masterpieces such as *The Gates of Hell, The Burghers of Calais* and *The Thinker*. In the light and spacious house, Rodin's own works including *The Kiss* are displayed alongside his own wonderful collection of art, including works by Van Gogh, Renoir, Monet, and extraordinary sculptures that were crafted by his lover and muse, Camille Claudel.

PAGE 104 *Rodin's statue* The Thinker *is just one of several of his world-famous works on display at the Musée Rodin*

FAR LEFT *Inside the museum Rodin's works are on display, in situations similar to when the mansion was his studio*

LEFT *The grounds contain both familiar and unfamiliar Rodin works, but every one showing the touch of his genius*

Tour Eiffel

ABOVE *The Eiffel Tower may be more familiar from a distance, but a close-up view reveals an angle that shows its structural beauty*

OPPOSITE *Today the tower is as much a part of the Paris skyline as is the dome of the Panthéon, appearing to stand in front of it*

Whether you see it as a 'hollow candlestick' or an elegant emblem of an elegant city, you just can't ignore the Eiffel Tower. Its sleek iron silhouette somehow seems to find its way into many of the city's best views. By night and by day, from above and below, from near or from a distance, the Eiffel Tower is impressive, beautiful, powerful, and a unique symbol for this unique city. There is no place like Paris, and nothing can compare to the Eiffel Tower. No matter how familiar it is, it can never be ignored. To return to the city and see it again is like meeting up with an old friend, but one who remains unchanged in an ever-changing world.

About 17,000 people visit the tower every single day of the year, coming from every continent to take its photo and catch the elevator ride to the top. Well, almost to the top of its 1,063ft (324m), and it can even be a little higher

on hot days when the metal expands. So solid is Gustave Eiffel's structure, that on the windiest days the top of the tower never sways more than about 4.5 inches (12cm). Even during the fierce storms that battered France in 1999 and uprooted trees and blew down houses, the tower was only recorded as swaying by 3.5 inches (9cm).

Facts and figures about the tower can't help but fascinate, as we attempt to make sense of its size and scale, and the engineering feat behind it. It weighs 10,100 metric tons, which makes you wonder at the logistics of bringing so much metal to the banks of the Seine in the centre of Paris. There are 18,000 separate metal parts, held together by 2.5 million rivets, which must have been good news for rivet-makers in 1889.

The lifts that were also built in 1889 are still in operation, travelling between them about 62,000 miles

(100,000km) a year, taking the tower's six million annual visitors up and down between the three different levels. Some escape the queues by climbing the 360 steps from the ground to the first level, and if not exhausted you can continue to climb another 700 steps to the second level, to then take one of the small lifts that goes up to the third-level viewing gallery. Here you are 918ft (280m) in the air, and on clear days the view extends for about 50 miles (80km) around Paris. The views are often at their best at the run-up towards sunset, when the light is kinder to cameras. At night a totally different picture unfolds, as hundreds of thousands of lights sketch out the city. This was a view enjoyed by Gustave Eiffel once the tower was nearing completion, as he had an office up here; you can see a reconstruction of his sitting room.

It was in 1889 that Eiffel began enjoying the views, and seeing his audacious vision becoming a reality. He had been commissioned to build the tower for the 1889 Universal Exhibition, and it took two years to construct, only just meeting the deadline. In fact for the opening ceremony the lifts still weren't ready, and Eiffel and the city officials had to climb 1,665 steps to the top.

The tower was not universally admired, and was criticized by some notable people including Émile Zola and Guy de Maupassant. It was de Maupassant who said bitterly that he enjoyed dining at the Eiffel Tower as it was the only place in the city where he didn't have to look at it. But where writers opposed it, artists including Utrillo, Dufy and Pissarro all praised it, and it was the artists whose opinions were vindicated. The tower was only intended to stand for only 20 years, but by the time its allotted two decades were up it had as many dedicated fans as it had opponents. It was eventually saved simply for its broadasting antennae, and it gained another 66ft (20m) in 1957, when TV antennae were added to the top.

Famous visitors to the Eiffel Tower have included Thomas Edison, King George VI and his wife Queen Elizabeth (later to become the Queen Mother) and the Shah of Persia.

It remained the tallest building in the world until the New York's Chrysler Building came along in 1930, and has become the symbol of Paris and one of the most distinctive buildings in the world.

OPPOSITE *The tower casts a long shadow over the Paris cityscape, reaching across the river to touch the gardens of the Palais de Chaillot*

BELOW *Captured in miniature, the distinctive shape of the Eiffel Tower allows visitors to take a little bit of Paris home with them*

OVERLEAF *The vast dramatic design of the tower can be appreciated from yet another angle*

The Champs-Élysées & Chaillot

The most famous street in Paris, the Champs-Élysées, is the one everyone wants to walk along when they visit the city. It no longer carries quite the glamour that its name evokes, being lined now by car showrooms and chain stores rather than chic pavement cafés and elegant boutiques, but it is still the street that fills with people when Parisians want to celebrate an event, such as winning the World Cup, welcome a visitor, as with the annual finish of the Tour de France, or mourn the passing of a great leader, like General de Gaulle.

From the Arc de Triomphe at the top, the street runs down to the place de la Concorde, and around it several palaces indicate the area's importance, including the Palais de l'Élysée, which was built in 1718 and is now where the French President lives.

By contrast, the Chaillot quarter, which stands between the Arc de Triomphe and the river, was still a village until as late as the 19th century. Then, in the building boom overseen by the Emperor Napoleon III and his architect Baron Haussmann, Chaillot was transformed, like the rest of the city, with wide boulevards and grand new mansions. It gained its own palace when the Palais de Chaillot was constructed in 1878, and now it's a district of embassies, expensive restaurants and exclusive addresses.

Even a familiar Paris sight like the Arc de Triomphe reveals hidden beauty when seen from another angle

Arc de Triomphe

Napoleon's Triumphal Arch has been a Paris landmark, and rallying point, since 1836. Napoleon himself did not live to see its completion as he died 15 years before it was finally unveiled. He had conceived the arch in 1806 to celebrate his victory the previous year in the Battle of Austerlitz, but his subsequent fall from grace and other problems delayed its completion. He died in 1821 in exile on Saint Helena, but in 1840 his remains were returned to France and his funeral procession passed beneath the Arc de Triomphe.

The arch stands in one of the busiest squares in the city, where 12 roads merge to form a gigantic and ever-busy traffic junction known as l'Étoile, the Star. The arch is also the spot where the Tomb of the Unknown Soldier can be found, a tribute to those who died during World War I. It was erected in 1920 and the Memorial Flame was added in 1923. Today it is re-ignited every evening at 6:30pm.

The arch is open to the public, and inside there is a small shop and museum. Steps or a lift take visitors to the roof, 164ft (50m) high, from which there are wonderful views, especially down the Champs-Élysées to place de la Concorde. Looking to the east the Arc de Triomphe lines up with the Arc de Triomphe du Carrousel, outside the Louvre, and looking west it is in line with the Grande Arche at La Défense. This line is known as the Grand Axis, with the Arche at La Défense being twice as big as the Arc de Triomphe, which in turn is twice as big as the arch in front of the Louvre.

OPPOSITE Up close the sculptures on the Arc de Triomphe can be appreciated, none more striking nor proudly French than La Marsellaise

BELOW No matter how many times the visitor to Paris has seen the Arc de Triomphe in photographs and on film, the first sight of the real thing, especially spectacularly lit like this at night, is inspiring

Champs-Élysées

The 'Elysian Fields' runs for about 1.2 miles (2km) down from the Arc de Triomphe (from the top of which you can look along its entire length) to the Egyptian obelisk that stands in the centre of the place de la Concorde. The street is a uniform 232ft (71m) wide, and dates back originally to 1616, when Marie de Médici decided to turn the area into fashionable driveway of trees leading from the Tuileries Palace. In those days this part of the city was a mix of marshland, market gardens and rural fields.

In 1667 a decision was made to further improve and extend this stretch, and the acclaimed architect and landscape gardener André le Nôtre was hired to design the street, which was completed in 1670. It was then called Grand-Cours (the Great Way), and the name was changed to the Champs-Élysées in the early 18th century. Various other improvements and extensions were made both on the street and in the Jardins des Champs-Élysées at the eastern end. These incorporate the Palais de l'Élysée, the official residence of the French President, the Grand Palais and the Petit Palais.

In the days of the Second Empire, in the late 19th century, the Champs-Élysées became known as a hugely fashionable place to stroll, to see and be seen, and the street's reputation for stylishness continued well into the 20th century. Pavement cafés were opened and were packed with Parisians, especially at weekends. In recent years it has become a much more commercially minded street, very much like main streets in cities all round the world, with record shops, souvenir stalls, chain stores, airline offices and car showrooms.

The French come here to celebrate, whether it be winning the soccer World Cup or welcoming participants in the Tour de France cycle race. The avenue has hosted some of France's most prestigious processions, including General de Gaulle's Liberation March in 1944 and the bicentenary celebrations of the French Revolution in 1989.

A handful of the pavement cafés are still there, offering some of the most expensive coffee in Paris, and cheaply dressed tourists now easily outnumber chic Parisians, but a stroll along the Champs-Élysées is still as much a part of anyone's first visit to Paris as a trip to the Eiffel Tower. A particularly good time to visit this famous street is during the Christmas illuminations.

ABOVE *Lamps and awnings decorate buildings along the Champs-Élysées while on upper floors are the human touches of hanging baskets of flowers*

RIGHT *Non-stop traffic along the Champs-Élysées and around the Arc de Triomphe is a constant sight, day or night*

Grand Palais

The Grand Palais was built for the Universal Exhibition of 1900, along with the Petit Palais and the Pont Alexandre III, which links the Grand Palais and Petit Palais in a straight line with Les Invalides and Napoleon's Tomb on the far side of the Seine. This exhibition is the one for which the Gare d'Orsay was opened (see pages 78-83), to bring the increased numbers of visitors into the city.

What those visitors found was a city developing at a fast pace. The Eiffel Tower was 11 years old, and the new Grand Palais was an imposing site, its soaring domes of glass and steel representing typical Parisian architecture. Illuminated at night it looked – and still looks – like some vast greenhouse from a giant's garden, or something descended from outer space. Like the Eiffel Tower, neither of the two new Palais were intended to be permanent, and yet they shape the face of the Paris that we know today.

Part of the Grand Palais is given over to temporary exhibitions, while the western side houses the science museum, the Palais de la Découverte. This owes its existence to the 1937 World's Fair held in Paris. It's very hands-on, and very much aimed at children, covering traditional topics such as electricity and physics and more modern scientific subjects like climate change and nuclear power. The latest fibre-optic technology is used to present realistic views of outer space, every bit as ground-breaking as the building of the Grand Palais was in its day.

RIGHT The sight of the Grand Palais illuminated at night and from across the river reveals just what a remarkable structure it is

BELOW The intimate detail of one of the nearby bridges across the River Seine

Jardin des Tuileries

Tucked between the River Seine and the rue de Rivoli, the Tuileries is not the most peaceful park in Paris but being so central is easily one of the most visited. It's very much an urban park, with the noise of the traffic hard to escape, but it is still a popular place for locals to take a break, where children can play, and where visitors can get good views of several of the city's main attractions. There are good views of the Louvre, the Eiffel Tower, the Musée d'Orsay across the river and up to the Arc de Triomphe standing at the top of the Champs-Élysées.

The formal design of the gardens can be credited to the landscape architect André le Nôtre, who was gardener to King Louis XIV and the man responsible for the spectacular gardens at Versailles. Le Nôtre laid out the Tuileries in 1664, and over 300 years later they are still being enjoyed. In one corner is a boating pond, and at the opposite end overlooking the place de la Concorde are two of the city's finest small galleries, the Orangerie and the Jeu de Paume. The latter gets its name from the fact that it was once a real tennis court (*jeu de paume*) and the former (see pages 42-43) a warm winter home for the orange trees from the Jardin. There is plenty of art in the gardens too. Works by Giacometti, Rodin and Henry Moore are on display, and several bronzes by Maillol.

ABOVE *The colourful beauty of the flowers in the Jardin des Tuileries can often be overlooked among the park's many other attractions*

LEFT *The sculptures in the grounds include 18 works by Aristide Maillol as well as pieces by Henry Moore, Giacometti and Max Ernst, with around 100 statues on display in the gardens altogether*

BELOW *Visitors envious of children sailing their boats in the pond can rent a boat and still have their fun*

Palais de Chaillot

For a first breathtaking view of the Eiffel Tower, the terraces of the Palais de Chaillot are hard to beat as a vantage point. If you arrive at night, when the tower is illuminated, it's a sight never to be forgotten. A photograph can record the scene, but it can never quite capture the thrill inside.

This has been a desirable spot since long before the tower was even a twinkle in Eiffel's eye. Napoleon hoped to build a palace here for his son, but he fell from grace before this could happen. The first palace was built on this natural little hill overlooking the river in 1878 for the Universal Exhibition, and was replaced by the present building for the 1937 Universal Exhibition. Below the terraces is the Théâtre National de Chaillot, and the palace's wings house two museums, the Musée National de la Marine and Le Cité de l'Architecture et du Patrimoine.

The City of Architecture and Patrimony tells the story of French architecture down the years. There are examples of French buildings from the Middle Ages onwards, and the museum also covers modern French architecture, of which there are many fine examples around Paris. The National Maritime Museum is one of the largest in the world, and was begun by King Charles X in 1827. There are some fine paintings of French ships, beautifully crafted naval instruments and, best of all, numerous model ships whose craftsmanship just has to be admired.

Outside, it's the craftsmanship and grace of the Eiffel Tower rising up into the clouds which most people come to admire. It's an important gathering place on New Year's Eve, when the city usually puts on a special *son et lumière* show, and again on Bastille Day, when there are plenty of impressive fireworks. To appreciate it from a number of angles you can walk down through the Jardins du Trocadéro, which stand between the Palais and the Seine and whose fountains, statues and pond make marvellous settings for more photographs of the tower.

ABOVE *The Palais and its terraces provide one of the best places in the city from which to see the Eiffel Tower, especially at night or on Bastille Day, when there are huge firework displays*

FAR LEFT *One of the gold statues that line the front of the Palais de Chaillot, built during the 1937 Exposition Internationale in the place du Trocadéro*

Palais de l'Élysée

Only a handful of chosen people are invited to see inside the Élysée Palace, official residence of the French President and therefore closed to the public. Visiting politicians, royalty and other notables may be lucky enough to get an invitation, and over the years its distinguished guests have included Queen Victoria, the Duke of Wellington and Napoleon Bonaparte.

It was a very familiar place to Napoleon, as it was for a time the home of his sister, Caroline Murat. Later, his wife, the Empress Josephine, would call it home, and Bonaparte's nephew Napoleon III also lived at this distinguished address in 1851. By 1873 it had become the official home of the French President. The palace was first built in 1718 as a private house for the Count of Évreux,

BELOW *Kings and queens, presidents and dukes, all have entered the doors of the Élysée Palace over the centuries, since it was built as a private mansion, the Hôtel d'Évreux, in 1718*

and was then owned by the Marquise de Pompadour, whose rather better-known wife Madame de Pompadour became Louis XV's mistress. She was responsible for enlarging the building and extending the gardens at the rear down to the Champs-Élysées.

After the French Revolution the palace became a state printing works and then for a time was a dance hall, and then a restaurant and the site of a fairground, before becoming witness to many political dances over the years.

French ministers meet here every Wednesday in the council chamber, the Salon Murat, while the public have the chance to see this room and some of the rest of the building just once a year. On the third weekend in September the annual Journées du Patrimoine (Patrimony Days) allow free admission into buildings normally closed to the public. The Presidential Palace is one of the most popular of these, and queues start forming early to get a look inside the house their President calls home.

ABOVE *French flags fly at the Élysée Palace, marking it as the official residence of the French President*

Petit Palais

The Petit Palais was built at the same time as its grander
neighbour, the Grand Palais, for the 1900 Paris Exposition.
The domed Petit Palais was designed by Charles Girault,
and was intended to echo the look of Les Invalides (see
pages 98-101) across the River Seine.

The two palaces are connected to the Hôtel des
Invalides in a direct line across the river over the Pont
Alexandre III. This was also built especially for the 1900
Exposition, to allow easier access to the two new palaces
from the Left Bank. The foundation stone was laid by
Alexandre III of Russia. When the Exposition of 1900

was finished, part of the Petit Palais became home in 1902
to the Musée des Beaux-Arts de la Ville de Paris. This
collection of fine arts remains at the Petit Palais, a suitable
home for the furniture, sculpture, jewellery, ceramics and
other beautiful objects.

The paintings on display include works by Cézanne,
Rembrandt, Ingres, Pissarro, Tissot, Courbet, Poussin,
Géricault and Monet. The porcelain collection includes
work from China as well as Meissen and Sèvres, and there
are sculptures by Renoir and Rodin, ceramics by Gauguin
and glass and jewellery by Lalique and Tiffany.

LEFT *Sweeping stairways in the Petit Palais show it to be a superb setting for works by some of the world's finest artists, including Tiffany, Lalique, Rembrandt, Renoir and Rodin*

BELOW *At the entrance to the Petit Palais, a statue of the British wartime leader Winston Churchill seems to stride towards the street named in his honour: avenue Winston Churchill*

OPPOSITE *The Egyptian obelisk at the centre of the place de la Concorde dates back to the 8th century BC, making it Paris's oldest monument*

LEFT *The fountains in the place de la Concorde are copies of those in St Peter's Square in Rome, and contain figures representing navigation by land and by sea*

BELOW *These elaborately decorated lamp-posts can be found on the east side of the place de la Concorde*

Place de la Concorde

As traffic swirls around the largest square in Paris, and people enjoy the pedestrian area in the centre, it's hard to imagine that this was once swamp land on the edge of the city. It didn't become a square until the late 18th century, as it was laid out between 1755 and 1775 by Jacques-Ange Gabriel in order to display an equestrian statue of the king, Louis XV. Gabriel also designed two of the principal buildings overlooking the square, the exclusive Hôtel Crillon and the Hôtel de la Marine, which help to give it a feeling of harmony, though the name 'Concorde' came much later.

The square was originally named after the king, place Louis XV, but during the French Revolution it was renamed place de la Révolution and the statue of the king was taken down and replaced by the guillotine. King Louis

XVI and Marie Antoinette were just two of over 1,300 people who were beheaded here between 1793 and 1795. It was after these bloody events that the square was renamed yet again as place de la Concorde, as a hopeful gesture to the future.

The square's most visible feature is the Egyptian obelisk which stands at its centre. This was given to King Louis-Philippe in 1833 by Mohammed Ali, the Viceroy of Egypt. It is made of pink granite, is over 3,000 years old, 75ft (23m) high, weighs 230 tonnes and once stood in the Temple of Thebes in present-day Luxor. In each corner of the octagonal place de la Concorde are eight 18th-century stone pavilions, each carrying a female statue representing one of the French provincial capitals: Lille, Strasbourg, Lyons, Marseilles, Bordeaux, Nantes, Brest and Rouen.

GSON
UNEL
SCHAL

LA DIAPHANE
Poudre de Riz
SARAH BERNHARDT
32, Avenue de l'Opéra PARIS

aris

ert

SAMEDIS

MONTMARTRE

Palai
de GI

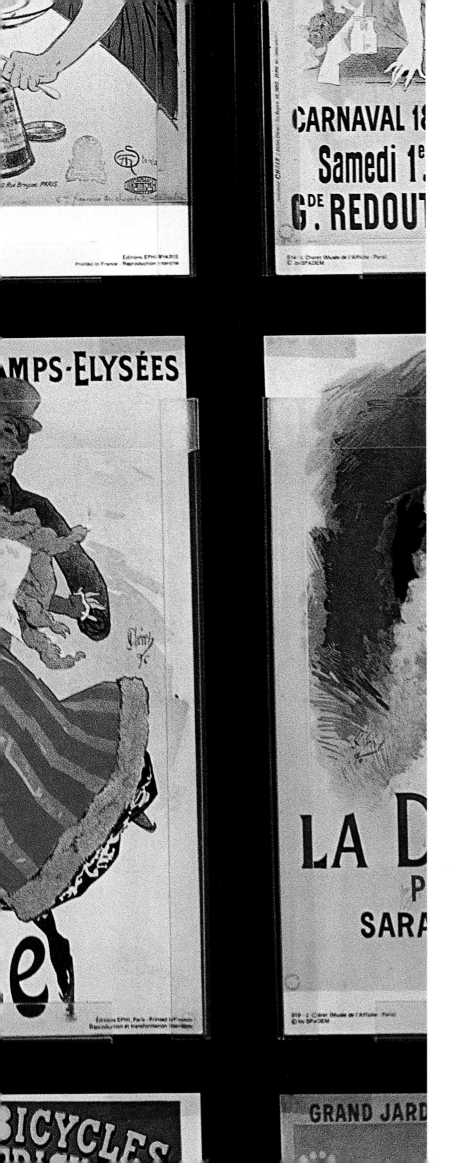

Montmartre

There is nowhere in the world like Montmartre. It may no longer be the hilly village on the edge of the city, frequented by artists and showgirls who flitted in and out of the clubs and cabarets like the Moulin Rouge, but it still retains its unique character. You may not find it in the modern commerciality of the place du Tertre, where artists do lightning sketches of the tourists who flock there, but a wander up and down the cobbled streets north and west of here will help recapture some of that Bohemian atmosphere.

There is an air of rakishness and eccentricity about Montmartre, which can still feel like a village set apart from the rest of Paris. It is the only place in Paris that still has a vineyard, and every year when the grapes are in and the annual vintage is bottled, a great street party follows, with the wine being auctioned for charity – and then immediately drunk. In ways like this the spirit of Montmartre lives on, and particularly in the place des Abbesses, where locals enjoy the café life, unbothered by too many tourists.

Cabarets like the Moulin Rouge and Au Lapin Agile still exist too, and some of the houses, apartments and studios where artists like Van Gogh, Picasso, Utrillo, Toulouse-Lautrec, Renoir, Monet, Dali and many others lived and worked can still be seen. Some of the feeling of that period in the late 19th and early 20th centuries were best captured in the vivid posters produced by Toulouse-Lautrec showing some of the dancers and cabaret-goers. These posters now hang on the walls of galleries like the Musée d'Orsay, prized as priceless works of art and portraits of a special period in the city's history.

These colourful posters capture perfectly the joie de vivre of 19th-century Paris

Moulin Rouge

There was never a real moulin rouge – a red windmill – here in the hilly streets of Montmartre, although working windmills did once turn their sails on the heights to the north of the city.

The Moulin Rouge opened as a cabaret in 1889 and quickly gained a racy reputation for its cancan dancing girls and other scantily clad showgirls, who often worked for the area's starving artists as still-life models during the daytime. The cancan wasn't a new dance, it had been around for many years, but it was its introduction as a special number at the Moulin Rouge that brought it to the attention first of French society and later to the world. Some of the dancers were trained ballerinas, who were able to use their skills to great effect in a very physically demanding dance.

The cancan girls are still there today, albeit now as part of an expensive evening dinner cabaret show, catering to coach parties of visitors keen to get a glimpse of this side of Parisian life. Over the years, many famous singers have made guest appearances on the Moulin Rouge stage, including Edith Piaf, Frank Sinatra, Liza Minnelli and Elton John. Some of the best-known dancers included La Goulue, with her dancing partner, nicknamed the Boneless Man, and Jane Avril, both of whom were captured on stage and in their quieter backstage moments by the artist Toulouse-Lautrec. The American-born singer and entertainer Josephine Baker, the Black Pearl, also made a name for herself here.

The Moulin Rouge's legend was enhanced by the 2001 musical film *Moulin Rouge,* which starred Nicole Kidman and Ewan McGregor. There had already been a film of the same title made in 1952, which was an adaptation of a book by French author Pierre La Mure about the life of Toulouse-Lautrec. Both films were nominated for Academy Awards, and caught the spirit of the Moulin Rouge in their very different ways.

ABOVE *The neon sails of the Moulin Rouge, the 'red windmill', draw fun-seekers to the cabaret door*

RIGHT *Captured countless times in print, on film and on canvas, the Moulin Rouge conjures up an almost mythical Paris of romance, dance, art and passion*

Place des Abbesses

The metro station at place des Abbesses is probably the most photographed metro station in Paris, as its art nouveau entrance has an elegance and style that sums up the city for many people. At one time most of the metro station entrances looked like this, designed by architect Hector Guimard, with ornate wrought-iron arches, lanterns and, on the top, a ship shield, which is the symbol of Paris.

This entrance at the place des Abbesses is a rare survivor to be treasured. The only other like it is at Porte Dauphine. It marks the entrance to the deepest metro station in Paris, the platform being about 300ft (91m) below street level. If the elevator isn't working, it's a climb of 285 steps up or down. Despite its recognizability, it isn't the original metro entrance as it was moved here from the Hôtel de Ville only in 1970.

It is here on this square rather than at the place du Tertre that is the focus of Montmartre life today. It could be said that the place du Tertre is for visitors, while the place des Abbesses is for residents to enjoy. They can be found in the pavement cafés and chatting under the trees that line the square, for all the world as if they were in a quiet French village somewhere.

The whole area around here is called Abbesses, and the name comes from the fact that there was an abbey here in medieval times. This being Montmartre, though, it was no ordinary abbey as in 1590 the abbess was rumoured to have had an affair with Henri of Navarre, who was later to become King Henri IV. Only in Montmartre...

RIGHT *Once the signs for most Paris Métro stations looked like this, but today only two remain and one is here at the place des Abbesses*

BELOW *Montmartre's famous Wall of Love*

Place du Tertre

Standing almost literally in the shadow of Sacré-Coeur, today's place du Tertre is home to lightning-sketch artists dashing off amusing portraits of the visitors who have come to see the Basilica and get a glimpse of Montmartre. What they won't glimpse is the history of the square, though Maison Catherine at number 6 could certainly tell them a tale or two. The restaurant has been here since 1793 and is said to have been where the word 'bistro' originated. Russian troops were stationed here in 1814 and tried to hurry up the service by shouting 'bystro!' ('quickly' in Russian) to the waiters. However, as the soldiers dined all over Paris, and the word probably didn't enter the French language until the 1880s, it may well be a fanciful story. It wouldn't be the first in Montmartre.

Not that there aren't any number of real stories about this square, whose name can be more believably explained as *tertre* is French for a hillock, and place du Tertre is said to be Paris's highest natural point. It was certainly a good place for a scaffold. There used to be an abbey here, and the scaffold was there to punish anyone who disobeyed the Abbey's rules, which seems rather severe for a Christian order. One of the rules was that the owner of each local vineyard – and there used to be many here, though only one remains – had to give a quarter of his annual production to the Abbey by way of tax.

The artists have been here only since the 19th century, when Montmartre began to turn into a lively haunt for Bohemian painters with a love of cheap but strong absinthe; those who didn't meet at the place des Abbesses (see pages 134-35) would meet here at the place du Tertre, which has always been filled with cafés and restaurants, while Sacré-Coeur looks on disapprovingly.

OPPOSITE *The vivid night colours of the place du Tertre make it look less like a photograph and more like a painting by one of the artists who congregate there in the daytime*

BELOW (LEFT AND RIGHT) *In the daylight the place du Tertre is dominated by the easels and canvases of artists who have used this Montmartre square as their base since the 19th century*

Sacré-Coeur

The story of the Basilica dedicated to the Sacred Heart goes back to the start of the Franco-Prussian War in 1870. It was a war that Prussia was expected to win easily, with French soldiers being sent to the slaughter. Two Catholic businessmen, Alexandre Legentil and Rohault de Fleury, promised to build a church dedicated to the Sacred Heart if the French armies would be spared. Despite a long siege of Paris, the Prussians did not invade the city and the expected carnage did not take place. The two businessmen kept their word and work on the church began in 1875. It was finished in 1914 but was not consecrated until 1919, because of World War I.

It became – and remains today – the second-highest point on the French skyline after the Eiffel Tower, and anyone feeling particularly energetic can climb to the top for views that are said to stretch for 18 miles (30km).

Even from ground level the views across Paris from here are among the best in the city, and the terraces in front of the church are a popular spot both for photographing and for being photographed.

Sacré-Coeur has been called a monstrosity, and likened to a wedding cake, but it is still one of the sights most associated with the city, and an essential stop on even the briefest visit to Paris. The interior is as impressive as the outside, and one of its most notable features is a huge golden mosaic covering 5,145 sq ft (475 sq m), one of the largest in the world. The belltower at the back of the church also contains one of the heaviest bells in the world, weighing almost 19 tons and called La Savoyarde, because it was gift from the Catholics from Savoy, when funds were being raised from all over France to create this unique and impressive building.

BELOW *The dome of the Basilica of Sacré-Coeur seems to peek over the Montmartre rooftops, as if trying to keep an eye on this area which has always had a risqué atmosphere*

PAGE 139 *The scrubbed-white stone of Sacré-Coeur looks suitably pure as its dome and towers soar heavenwards like a fairytale castle – though some say a wedding cake*

Eastern Paris

East of the city centre there seems to be more breathing space and an easier pace. From the bustle of place de la Bastille it's possible to leave the city behind and climb the steps to the Promenade Plantée. This garden in the sky, invisible from the street, has been created on top of old railway viaducts that once carried trains in and out of the city. The elongated park leads almost all the way to the Bois de Vincennes, one of many large, leafy parks that beautify the suburbs.

In the northeast, the Parc de la Villette spreads over 136 acres (55 hectares) of parkland and science museums have been built where slaughterhouses once stood. It shows how Parisians care about their environment. The city is something to be enjoyed, to be used creatively, to be re-invented for the benefit of everyone. It was President Mitterand who used the phrase *grands projets*, but Paris has always had great projects, whether it be cutting-edge design in the city centre, transforming run-down areas or creating new parks, libraries and offices in suitable places. Even cemeteries.

In its day the cemetery of Père-Lachaise was a *grand projet*. It is almost as big as the Parc de la Villette and was always planned as an open space that people could enjoy, as well as a burial place, when it was constructed in 1804. In a way it resembles a little town, with tree-lined cobbled streets, but with burial vaults instead of houses. It brings people from all over the world out to this corner in eastern Paris, to give them a taste of life, as much as of death, away from the familiar city centre.

Lac Daumesnil is one of several lakes in the Bois de Vincennes, the Vincennes Woods, which was first designated a park for use by Parisians by King Louis XV in 1731

Parc de la Villette

From 1867 until 1974 the city slaughterhouses stood in this part of Paris which, unsurprisingly, did not have a lot going for it. Then the abattoirs were torn down and in the 1980s the architect Bernard Tschumi planned the Parc de la Villette. The only building to escape destruction during this redevelopment was the glass cattle hall, a huge glass and steel building which is now La Grande Halle, a space for concerts and trade shows. The whole park covers 136 acres (55 hectares), making it one of the largest scientific and cultural parks in the world.

On sunny days people often visit the park to enjoy the walkways, picnic areas, outdoor sculptures and children's playgrounds, without even going into any of the big museums here. The Cité des Sciences et de l'Industrie is a vast exploration of technology and industry, on several levels, including a planetarium aquarium, a movie theatre, a creative play area for children in the basement, a multimedia library, a health village, and that's without taking account of the several floors of hands-on displays that help children explore the main themes.

The Géode is another gigantic creation, like a shiny steel boules ball that is 118ft (36m) across, inside which is a cinema screen covering a surface area of almost 11,000 sq ft (1,000 sq m). At the far end of the park is the Cité de la Musique, which includes the Musée de la Musique. In here there are over 900 musical instruments on display, which visitors can listen to using wireless headphones. The Cité also explores every aspect of music, including models of the world's concert halls, and naturally it has its own concert performances, while outside in the grounds there may be buskers or musicians practising, adding to the delight of a day out in the Parc de la Villette.

OPPOSITE *Inside the steel Géode is a huge Omnimax cinema screen covering half the circular surface*

ABOVE *The Parc de la Villette is one of the newest Paris parks, created in the 1980s by the innovative archtect Bernard Tschumi*

Cimetière du Père-Lachaise

Père François de la Chaise, a Jesuit priest who had the distinction of being the confessor of King Louis XIV in the 17th century, once owned land here and was fond of visiting a home for retired priests that stood on the land. When the area was developed as a cemetery and public space in 1803, designed in the style of an English garden, it was named after him, though for a time the cemetery wasn't a popular resting place at all, until some notable

BELOW The tree-lined cobbled streets of the cemetery of Père-Lachaise give it something of the look of a quiet, French country town in miniature

graves were moved here, including those of Molière, and the lovers Abélard and Héloïse. Following this, it quickly became one of the most fashionable places in Paris in which to be buried. It has retained its cachet as a final resting place to this day, and the roll-call of the famous who lie in the ground here just goes on and on: Marcel Proust, Oscar Wilde, Baron Haussmann, Chopin, Bizet, Balzac, Ingres, Stéphane Grappelli, Edith Piaf, Maria

Callas, Modigliani, Isadora Duncan, Richard Wright, Gertrude Stein, Rossini, Géricault, Yves Montand, Simone Signoret and Colette.

One of the most visited graves today is that of the American singer Jim Morrison, of the cult rock group *The Doors*. Curious tourists come to see the latest offerings by his fans; indeed the grave had been receiving so much attention (and graffiti) that it was necessary to put a security guard on it. By way of contrast, there are touching memorials to people who were far from famous – the

victims of the Nazi concentration camps, for example, and the heroes of the French Resistance who fought for their country's freedom during World War II.

One of the best days for visiting Père-Lachaise is on 1 November, All Saints Day, when all the graves and burial vaults are adorned with flowers brought here to honour the famous and the ordinary dead alike. More like a park than a graveyard, this sought-after 19th-century resting place of celebrities is a tranquil haven in the heart of the bustling metropolis of Paris.

BELOW *The famous names who have been buried at Père-Lachaise include the Irish writer Oscar Wilde, whose tomb attracts admirers every day of the year*

Montparnasse

Wherever you are in Paris you can usually tell where the district of Montparnasse is, thanks to the huge Tour Montparnasse that juts up into the sky, not to the delight of everyone. In fact the whole area of Montparnasse has suffered from recent uninspiring development, showing that not even Paris always gets it right.

In the 1920s and 1930s Montparnasse was a little like a southern version of Montmartre, as it attracted writers such as Ernest Hemingway and artists including Modigliani and Marc Chagall. Some of its cultural appeal over the centuries can be seen in a few of the names buried in its cemetery: Maupassant, Baudelaire, Samuel Beckett, Jean-Paul Sartre, Simone de Beauvoir, Ionesco, Serge Gainsbourg, Jean Seberg and Man Ray.

The sculptor Émile-Antoine Bourdelle, who was a pupil of Rodin's, lived and worked in Montparnasse and his home is now a museum, on the street that's now been named after him: rue Antoine Bourdelle. Rodin himself also once lived here, as did Rilke, Gauguin, Modigliani, Whistler and Henri Cartier-Bresson.

For many people, though, Montparnasse is known simply as the name of one of the city's main railway terminuses. It's a huge and confusing station, but has hidden delights such as the garden on its roof. The Montparnasse district has its own hidden delights too, for anyone who takes the trouble to search them out. Some of those 1920s and 1930s haunts of artists and writers still exist, and there continues to be a thriving cultural life, perhaps all the more authentic for the fact that Montparnasse still just isn't fashionable.

It is not hard to see why the modern lines of the Tour Montparnasse are not universally popular, as it stands in stark contrast to much of the rest of the Paris skyline

147

Gare Montparnasse

Montparnasse is definitely not the prettiest place in Paris, and likewise its train station is far from being the most appealing of the city's railway terminuses. Although it's located in the south of the city, its tracks swing around and head west to serve Brittany and France's Atlantic coast. It's an extremely busy station, with a huge number of daily incoming services, and some of the attempts to improve it over the years have served to make it only more confusing. To take a few steps inside its main hall during the rush hour can often be like seeing a modern industrial version of Dante's *Inferno*.

However, there is escape from this chaos just a minute or two away, and it is visible only from above – the secret garden of the Gare Montparnasse. Parisians love their parks and gardens, and any aerial photo of the city will show apartment blocks with roof gardens and balconies crammed with greenery. Above the Gare Montparnasse the city planners created in 1995 the Jardin de l'Atlantique, named for the Atlantic coast that the trains here serve.

To find the garden is a little exploration in itself, as you need to walk down one or other of the main roads that run either side of the station and look for stairs leading up, the

garden being open from dawn till dusk every day. Suspended 60ft (18m) above the tracks is a little city park, complete with tennis courts, benches, pathways and some meteorological instruments as it is also used as a weather station. The instruments look like some futuristic sculpture right in the centre of the park. The trees and plants that are grown here are all from the Atlantic coast.

At the station end of the Jardin is the Musée Jean-Moulin, which tells the story of the revered French Resistance leader, Jean Moulin, whose name is remembered in streets and squares all over France. As leader of a secret army of fighters, this secret garden seems an appropriate place in which to commemorate him.

Tour Montparnasse

While the secret garden above the Gare Montparnasse is hard to find, the nearby Tour Montparnasse opposite the station is impossible to miss. In 1973 the railway terminus was moved, and in its original spot Europe's largest office block was built. It is an unapologetically modern building, striking in its way, imposing and impressive, but it has never endeared itself to all Parisians. Not even the man who approved the project, President Georges Pompidou, was enamoured of the result. Taken on a helicopter tour to see the finished building, he is reported to have said, 'That's enough, we stop right there.'

To adapt Maupassant's comment about the Eiffel Tower, the top of the Tour Montparnasse is also thought of by many as the best place in the city as it's the only spot in Paris where you don't have to look at the tower. Instead, the beauty of the whole of the capital is spread out around you, with a fabulous view of the Eiffel Tower and other notable buildings including the Arc de Triomphe, Nôtre-Dame and Sacré-Coeur.

The first viewing platform is on the 56th floor of the building, which is 685ft (209m) high, about two-thirds the height of the Eiffel Tower. The lift takes visitors up to the top in just 38 seconds, and there is a small cinema there, exhibition space, and those with a head for heights can go on further to the 59th floor, to the highest open-air terrace in Paris, where the views are said to stretch for about 25 miles (40km).

Those are the only two floors open to the public, and offices take up the first 52 floors, where about 5,000 people work. The building weighs 120,000 tonnes and its foundations go down 230ft (70m) underground. The outside is a mix of glass, aluminium and bronze, and whether you like it or hate it, the Tour Montparnasse is now firmly fixed on the Parisian skyline.

La Défense

The area of La Défense, and its most striking building the Grande Arche, illustrate perfectly how Paris approaches its city planning, and how the past and the future are deliberately connected and blended. The very name La Défense links back to the Franco-Prussian War in 1870, when French soldiers, despite being heavily outnumbered, made a heroic stand to defend the city against the Prussian army.

The history of La Défense goes back to 1958, when it was decided to develop the district to the west of the city for business and government offices, in order (amongst other things) to keep high-rise buildings out of the city centre. The first buildings date from the 1960s, and work has continued over the decades so that it has more or less become a living museum of late 20th-century architecture, but the cutting-edge designs always look to the future.

Today about 150,000 people work in the buildings at La Défense, and about 20,000 people call the district home. Most of the central area is pedestrianized, and the focus is the Grande Arche, which was opened in 1989 for the Bicentenary of the French Revolution.

Parisians always remember the past, even if they can't always be proud of it. The building of the Grande Arche, and its exact location and size, are part of a continuum linking La Défense with the city's historical and geographical centre. But go further back and there is another layer of history here in this futuristic spot, as it's located on Chantecoq Hill, where the patron saint of Paris, Geneviève, used to tend her sheep.

The futuristic area of La Défense is far from being most people's image of Paris, but it nevertheless reflects the stylish way in which the city quietly grows and embraces the new as well as the old

La Défense

The most notable feature of La Défense is the Grande Arche, the scale of which is hard to comprehend, even when you see it. It is wider than the Champs-Élysées and so high (360ft/110m) that Nôtre-Dame Cathedral could fit comfortably underneath it. The arch is a very simple open block structure that was one of President Mitterand's *grands projets*, and the design was chosen from 424 proposals that were submitted. The winner was Danish architect, Johan Otto von Spreckelsen, who sadly died before he could see his masterful creation completed.

The arch is in a direct line with the Arc de Triomphe, which can be seen 3.75 miles (6km) away, and hidden further on beyond that is the Arc du Carrousel outside the Louvre. The Grande Arche is about twice as high as the Arc de Triomphe, and reflects its simple shape, but up close it becomes clear that this is also a functional structure, as what appear at first sight to be solid walls actually contain working offices. The best view of the Arc de Triomphe is not from the top of the Grande Arche but from the top of the steps underneath it, while this view also provides a breathtaking feel of just how grand the Grande Arche is. Suspended from the Arche is an awning that resembles a cloud and provides some shade for the visitors on sunny days – which are good days to visit the complex, especially for photographers, as blue skies and bright light create stunning reflections and angular images around the whole area.

The Arche is constructed from 300,000 tonnes of concrete, glass and marble-cladding, supported on 12 pillars that go deep beneath the earth. Visitors can take a rather nerve-wracking ride in one of the external glass-bubble elevators to the top, where there is a viewing platform. From here you can see down what's called the Grand Axis to the Arc de Triomphe and beyond, while at another angle it becomes evident that the Grande Arche is also perfectly aligned with those other gigantic Paris constructions, the Eiffel Tower and the Tour Montparnasse, which stand one in front of the other.

OPPOSITE *The Grande Arche may be a long way in both distance and style from the Arc de Triomphe, but the vision of Paris as a city brings them together in harmony*

RIGHT *Modern flower-like sculptures add a whimsical touch to the sleek modern lines of the Grande Arche de La Défense*

ABOVE *Another view of the Grande Arche, framed by the bollowing cloud-like awning that is suspended through its centre*

OPPOSITE *The startling modern look of the buildings at La Défense is emphasized when the rays of the setting sun are at their strongest*

Although the Grande Arche is far and away the most spectacular sight at La Défense, there is a great deal else to see besides and there is even a train tour to take visitors round the buildings and sculptures during the summer months. Some of the most notable of the 50 or so public works of art are César's *The Thumb* and Joan Miró's *Figures*. Near to the Grande Arche is the huge CNIT Centre, an exhibition centre that boasts the world's largest concrete vaulted roof.

There are also fountains, cafés, restaurants, hotels and fashionable shopping centres, so La Défense, which is easy to reach on the metro and RER lines, makes for a good day out of the city centre. It's best visited during the week, when the offices are bustling and everything is open, and on summer evenings it's a popular and rather different place to linger, to enjoy a drink and a meal. A visit here is also a chance to reflect on the growth of such a remarkable

city, which continues to grow. West of La Défense, and created using some of the earth extracted during the building here, the Parc André Malraux covers 61 acres (25 hectares) and is the biggest park created in Paris since the dawn of the 20th century.

Think back too, to the grassy slopes of the Chantecoq Hill where St Geneviève grazed her sheep. By the late 19th century Napoleon III had extended the Champs-Élysées, which beyond the Arc de Triomphe becomes the avenue de la Grande Armée, all the way out to the hill and put up a statue of Napoleon I there. Later this was replaced by a statue commemorating the victory against the Prussians, La Défense de Paris. And now sheep and Napoleon and the statue have been succeeded by one of the most impressive developments in the history of this remarkable city, a city that celebrates its past while always looking to its future.

Index

Acknowledgements

The Automobile Association wishes to thank the following photographers and organizations for their assistance in the preparation of this book.

Abbreviations for the picture credits are as follows – (t) top; (b) bottom; (l) left; (r) right; (c) centre; (dps) double page spread; (AA) AA World Travel Library

1 AA/T Souter; 2/3 AA/J A Tims; 4/5 AA/B Rieger; 8/9 © Fernand Ivaldi/Iconica/Getty Images; 10 AA/T Souter; 10/1 AA/T Souter; 12/3 © Sylvain Sonnet/Photographer's Choice RR/Getty Images; 13 © Fernand Ivaldi/Photographer's Choice/Getty Images; 14 AA/C Sawyer; 15t AA/M Jourdan; 15b AA/M Jourdan; 16t AA/M Jourdan; 16b AA/K Paterson; 16/7 AA/J A Tims; 18 AA/C Sawyer; 18/9 AA/T Souter; 20 AA/M Jourdan; 21 AA/C Sawyer; 22/3 AA/M Jourdan; 24 © Dorling Kindersley/Getty Images; 24/5 © David Noton Photography/Alamy; 26 AA/T Souter; 26/7 AA/M Jourdan; 28 AA/C Sawyer; 29 AA/C Sawyer; 30tl © Patrick Ward/Alamy; 30bl © Peter Schneiter/Alamy; 31 AA/T Souter; 32/3 AA/J A Tims; 33 © Art Kowalsky/Alamy; 34 AA/M Jourdan; 35 AA/Phillip Enticknap; 36/7 AA/J A Tims; 38 AA/J A Tims; 39 AA/Phillip Enticknap; 40/1 AA/K Paterson; 41 AA/M Jourdan; 42/3 © JACQUES DEMARTHON/AFP/Getty Images; 43 AA/T Souter; 44 AA/M Jourdan; 44/5 AA/M Jourdan; 46/7 Pictures Colour Library; 48 AA/J A Tims; 48/9 © Martin Probert/Alamy; 50l AA/P Kenward; 50r AA/P Kenward; 51 AA/P Kenward; 52 AA/K Paterson; 53t AA/M Jourdan; 53bl AA/J A Tims; 53bc AA/K Paterson; 54 AA/T Souter, Picasso, Pablo © Succession Picasso/DACS 2008; 55 AA/M Jourdan, Picasso, Pablo © Succession Picasso/DACS 2008; 56/7 World Pictures/Photoshot; 57 © Danita Delimont/Alamy; 58 AA/P Kenward; 59 World Pictures/Photoshot; 60t AA/P Kenward; 60b © Tai Power Seeff/The Image Bank/Getty Images; 61 Eitan Simanor/Alamy; 62/3 AA/C Sawyer; 64 Pictures Colour Library; 65 © Combre Stephane/Alamy; 66 AA/B Rieger; 66/7 AA/M Jourdan; 68 AA/M Jourdan; 69 AA/M Jourdan; 70t AA/M Jourdan; 70b AA/M Jourdan; 71 © David A. Barnes/Alamy; 72/3 © Glenn Harper/Alamy; 73t © Bertrand Rieger/hemis.fr/Getty Images; 73b AA/T Souter; 74t AA/M Jourdan; 74b AA/K Paterson; 75 AA/C Sawyer; 76 © Louie Psihoyos/Science Faction/Getty Images; 76/7 © Tibor Bognar/Alamy; 78/9 AA/C Sawyer; 79 AA/T Souter; 80t © Peter Horree/Alamy; 80b © Peter Horree/Alamy; 81 AA/P Enticknap; 82 AA/M Jourdan; 82/3 World Pictures/Photoshot; 84l AA/J A Tims; 84r AA/J A Tims; 85 AA/K Paterson; 86t © Sandra Baker/Alamy; 86b © Max Alexander/ Dorling Kindersley/Getty Images; 87 Pictures Colour Library; 88 AA/M Jourdan; 89t AA/T Souter; 89b AA/M Jourdan; 90/1 AA/T Souter; 92 AA/P Kenward; 93 AA/P Kenward; 94 © Steve Frost/Alamy; 95 © Sylvain Sonnet/Photographer's Choice RR/Getty Images; 96l AA/J A Tims; 96r AA/B Rieger; 97 AA/K Paterson; 98/9 AA/K Paterson; 100 © Paul Miles/Alamy; 101t © Paul Miles/Alamy; 101b © FRED DUFOUR/AFP/Getty Images; 102 © Dag Sundberg/Photographer's Choice/Getty Images; 103 ©

cicciorillo/Alamy; 104 AA/M Jourdan; 105l AA/M Jourdan; 105r AA/M Jourdan; 106 AA/M Jourdan; 107 AA/B Rieger; 108 AA/M Jourdan; 108/9 AA/J A Tims; 110/11 AA/J A Tims; 112/3 AA/J A Tims; 114 AA/K Paterson; 115 AA/M Jourdan; 116 AA/C Sawyer; 116/7 AA/K Paterson; 118 AA/K Paterson; 118/9 AA/B Rieger; 120/1 AA/C Sawyer; 121tr AA/M Jourdan; 121b AA/C Sawyer; 122 AA/J A Tims; 122/3 AA/K Paterson; 124/5 World Pictures/Photoshot; 125 © PCL/Alamy; 126 © Renaud Visage/ Digital Vision/Getty Images; 127l © Directphoto.org/Alamy; 127r © FRANCOIS GUILLOT/AFP/Getty Images; 128 AA/K Paterson; 129t AA/B Rieger; 129b AA/P Kenward; 130/1 AA/T Souter; 132 AA/P Enticknap; 132/3 AA; 134 AA/C Sawyer; 134/5 AA/C Sawyer; 136 Pictures Colour Library; 137l World Pictures/Photoshot; 137r AA/C Sawyer; 138 AA/P Enticknap; 139 AA/T Souter; 140/1 World Pictures/Photoshot; 142 AA/M Jourdan; 143 AA/M Jourdan; 144/5 AA/M Jourdan; 145 AA/T Souter; 146/7 © David A. Barnes/Alamy; 148/9 © Kristina Williamson/Photonica/Getty Images; 149 © Eschcollection L / Alamy; 150 AA/C Sawyer; 151 AA/C Sawyer; 152/3 AA/B Rieger; 154 AA/K Paterson; 155 AA/J A Tims; 156 © allOver photography/Alamy; 156/7 © Justin Kase zonez/Alamy.

GATEFOLDS
Parks & Gardens
Gatefolds: 1 Montsouris Park, © Yann Layma/The Image Bank/Getty Images; 2l & r Champs Elysees, © Panoramic Images/Getty Images; 2cl People walk on the snow, 30 December 2005 in the Jardin des Tuileries, THOMAS COEX/AFP/Getty Images; 2cr Parisians enjoying a game of boules, AA/K Paterson.

Architectural Paris
Gatefolds: 1 Louvre Pyramid, © Panoramic Images/Getty Images; 2 l & r Paris Cityscape, © Harald Sund/Photographer's Choice/Getty Images; 2cl La Divette du Moulin cafe on Rue Lepic in Montmartre, AA/M Jourdan; 2cr Parc de la Villette, AA/M Jourdan.

Parisian Window
Gatefolds: 1 Saint Denis Cathedral, SIME/Ripani Massimo/4Corners Images; 2l & r Institut du Monde Arabe, Paris, AA/C Sawyer; 2cl Buildings reflected in Lavin shop window, 15 Faubourg St-Honore, AA/C Sawyer; 2cr Place de Vosges, AA/B Rieger; 2crb Faubourg St Honore in the Elysee area of Paris, AA/C Sawyer.

Romantic Paris
Gatefolds: 1 View across the Seine at sunset, towards the Cathedrale de Notre Dame, AA/P Enticknap; 2l & r Illuminated Eiffel tower, © Travelpix Ltd/Photographer's Choice/Getty Images; 2cl The Seine, Pont des Arts, AA/M Jourdan; 2cr Couple embracing on bench by River Seine, Anthony Harvie/Digital Vision/Getty Images.

Every effort has been made to trace the copyright holders, and we apologize in advance for any unintentional omissions or errors. We would be pleased to apply any corrections in any following edition of this publication.